# YORK MEMORIES
# AT HOME

Personal accounts of domestic life
in York, 1900-1960

**YORK ORAL HISTORY PROJECT
YORK CASTLE MUSEUM
1987**

# CONTENTS

| | |
|---|---:|
| INTRODUCTION | 4 |
| ACKNOWLEDGEMENTS | 6 |
| BIOGRAPHIES | 7 |
| WASHDAY AND IRONING | 9 |
| HOUSEHOLD CLEANING | 17 |
| COOKING AND BAKING | 25 |
| WOMEN WORKING | 30 |
| SHOPPING AND HOUSEHOLD ECONOMY | 34 |
| CHILDREN AND FAMILIES | 45 |
| HEALTH AND SICKNESS | 56 |
| CHRISTMAS | 61 |
| GAMES AND ENTERTAINMENT | 66 |

Spoken material © the contributors 1987
This collection © York Oral History Project.

Published jointly by York Castle Museum, York
and York Oral History Project
c/o Community House, 10 Priory Street, York.

Phototypeset, printed and bound by
Ryedale Printing Works Ltd, The Station, Helmsley, York. Tel: (0439) 70286.

ISBN 0 900264 18 7


Also available from York Oral History Project:

York Memories, Nine first-hand accounts of life in York 1900-1939.

York Memories At Work, Personal accounts of working life in York before 1952.

Front cover: West's Yard, Walmgate, in 1933. (Courtesy of the Northern Echo.)

# INTRODUCTION

History has often been handed down as a catalogue of political decisions and national events, or as a portrait gallery of the public figures who most *obviously* shaped society. However, over the past thirty years a growing number of social historians, history groups, and museums have shifted the focus of their studies to concentrate on the largely unwritten story of the majority. The participants in this new movement share a belief that the history of 'ordinary' people is not only absorbing in its own right, but also essential to an understanding of *our* society and its past. York Oral History Project has been recording the memories of York people for several years and has already published two collections, *York Memories* and *York Memories At Work*. *York Memories At Home* is concerned with domestic life and, given that homes and families are the centre of most people's lives, the subject is undoubtedly important. This book has been produced with the help of York Castle Museum and the union is a natural one which reunites the objects used by York people with their memories of them.

The people in this book are mainly women who ran their homes on limited budgets with minimal household technology. The patriarchal world of industry and commerce excluded many of them from paid work, as did the raising of children, but they worked in the home as part of an 'industrial revolution' which is still going on. The work was hard, often extremely hard, and several chapters in the book record this and show ways in which the work and the attitude towards it have changed. The interviews also cover aspects of domestic life which do not depend upon money or technology but upon people. Family life is described from several points of view: the relationships between children and parents, sisters and brothers, and wives and husbands are all discussed. These are first-hand accounts of how families made homes, how they spent their time together, and how children grew up and became parents themselves. Many of the people and places in this book have gone, but they survive in these memories to recreate the social world from which recognisable aspects of contemporary life in York have evolved. These memories are therefore a part of our inheritance and their preservation and publication are important.

If you are interested in oral history and would like further information we will be delighted to hear from you. York Oral History Project is a voluntary group and we always welcome new members. We can be contacted at the following address:

York Oral History Project
Community House
10 Priory Street
York YO1 1EZ

or Tel: (0904) 610028

## EDITORS

Ian Rayson, Pam Biggs, Sandra Butt, Sara Dickson, Elaine Dodds, Alan Hardwick, Michael Heather, Nita Heather, Alexander Johnson, Myrna Manning, Patrick Neal, Liz Ogborn, Sara Smoker, Mark Suggitt, Helen Tolhurst, Roy Wallington, Alex White and Margaret Williams.

Photography by John Lally.

# ACKNOWLEDGEMENTS

Obviously we owe our greatest debt to the people of York who allowed us to interview them, and to those who lent us photographs to be copied for our archive. Our work depends entirely upon the goodwill of local people.

In addition, York Oral History Project and York Castle Museum would like to thank the following:

 The College of Ripon & York St John

The Manpower Services Commission and the staff of The Community Programme in York.

The staff of York Council for Voluntary Service.

All the many individuals, groups and institutions who have supported our work in the past and who we hope will continue to do so in the future.

# BIOGRAPHIES

These short biographies are intended to help readers relate the memories in the book to other details of the contributors' lives. A knowledge of the contributors' dates of birth etc. can also help to identify which period is under discussion when the text does not make this clear.

**Mrs Armstrong** was born in the Bar Hotel, Micklegate in 1917. She left school at fourteen, qualified as a short-hand typist and worked for the NFU Mutual Insurance Society. After her marriage she stayed on as a part-time clerk until she retired in 1977 with forty-four years of service to her credit.

**Mr Armstrong** was born in St Anne Street in 1914. On leaving school he became a butcher's boy for two years before working as an assistant in a shoe shop and as a bus conductor. He joined the Post Office telephones branch in 1939 and stayed with them until he retired in 1974. He served in HM Forces between 1940-46.

**Miss Beswick** was born in 1906 and lived in Strensall as a child. Her father was a policeman. She attended Priory Street School in York. In her late teens she went away to nurse and worked in Southern Africa before returning to York.

**Mrs Burton** was born in Scarborough in 1899 and moved to York to live in Wilberfoss in 1925. She married her husband at Askham Bryan in 1926 and settled on a farm where they had three children. Also living on the farm were a number of farmhands and a domestic servant called Emma Johnson.

**Mrs Graham's** father was in the army and she was born at Fulford Barracks in 1914, the year he was killed at Ypres. She lived in Fulford until 1926 when her mother died. She then lived with and cared for her invalid aunt until she married in 1939. She has two daughters.

**Mrs Hadley** was born Mary Todd in 1918. Her father was on service with the Royal Navy and didn't see her until she was three years old. She left school at fourteen and worked as a telephonist, general clerk and wages clerk for Terry's. She was married in 1941, just before her husband served in India and Burma during the Second World War. During this time she joined the ATS as a wireless operator. After the war she brought up three children, and her husband worked for the Health Department. They are now retired and have six grandchildren.

**Miss Kirby** was born in 1891 and moved to York as a child. She worked all her life as a domestic servant, and is the only surviving member of a family of nine children.

**Mrs Moore** was born in 1895 in the Leeman Road area of York. Her mother kept a shop in Albany Street where she helped and worked. After its closure she worked at Rowntree's where she met her husband, whereupon she left work to bring up their three daughters. She has lived in Sycamore Terrace for over fifty years.

**Mrs Pilgrim** was born Dorothy Robson in 1912 at Huntington. Her mother was cook for the Archbishop of York. She worked as a hairdresser before bringing up her four children during the war. She and her husband now have nine grandchildren.

**Mr Pilgrim** was born in Malta in 1910 before living in the Wigginton Road area of York. His father was an army regular who died of war wounds in 1918. He worked in an office and then in the RAF.

**Miss Prentice** was born in 1905 in Hanover Street. In the 1920's she worked as a between-stairs maid at the Mansion House before becoming general maid at a boarding house in Grosvenor Terrace. In 1935 she married and lived in Scunthorpe for five years before moving back to live in Holgate Road. After the Second World War she worked during the evenings on the cash-desk of the Regent's Cinema.

**Mrs Rennison** was born in 1933 at the Ivy Dean Nursing Home in Acomb. Her parents were both York people, and her great-grandfather owned 'The Windmill' in Heslington. She worked in Rowntree's offices before marrying. She has four children and for the last eleven years has worked at Terry's.

**Mr Thomas** was born in 1901 in Bishopthorpe Road. His father was an engine driver and his mother a chamber-maid. After leaving school he qualified as an electrical engineer and worked for the General Post Office for most of his working life.

**Mrs Thomlinson** was born Vera Cass in 1916 and lived in Leeman Road during her childhood. She left school at fifteen and trained as a bakeress until she married in 1939. During the war she worked at Rowntree's and also fire-watched. She has two children and four grandchildren.

**Miss Worfolk** was born in Russell Street in 1910, and grew up in Bishopthorpe Road where her mother ran a women's and children's outfitters and haberdashery business. She was educated at Priory Street School and after an apprenticeship at Leak and Thorpe followed her mother's trade. She had her own business in Stonegate where she worked until retirement.

# WASHDAY AND IRONING

Before modern technology, laundering the household's clothes and linen was a very time consuming job. In this chapter the work is described and the difference made by modern equipment is discussed.

**Mrs Rennison**

Washday was always a Monday - it was always washing and ironing day, everything rolled into one. I can remember, mum used to get up at about six in the morning, and we had a copper in the corner of the yard with a sort of lean-to shed over it, and mum used to get up and light this thing. There used to be quite a rumpus if it wouldn't go - the sticks were wet, as she used to say, or the paper was damp. Washday used to take well into the afternoon because in those days you had to boil your whites; you used to get your water out of the copper to put into your wash-tub to start them off, and then, of course, all your whites were boiled in your copper. Oh I can still smell it - it was a lovely smell I thought. But our copper wasn't inside it was outside and, of course, there was the very old wooden roller-wringer in the lean-to as well and we used to think it was great helping with this thing - it was an enormous thing... And in those days, as I say, we used to try to get the ironing done. I remember coming in from school at teatime and there was mother ironing with the old flat-irons that you used to stick on the fire - you know, you'd spit on them to make sure they were hot and they used to 'siss'. [We had] a very old black range with an oven at one side, the fire in the middle, and then at the other side it was a sort of water-boiler although we never used it for hot water; it was always used for keeping the sticks dry 'cause me father chopped the sticks that went in there... Starching, that's another thing that's not really done now. I can remember the 'dolly bluebags' that you sort of held in your hand tightly, and just went like that quickly, because if you touched anything you'd get a blue mark - but it did sort of whiten your clothes. You'd not got to get too much in or everything came out blue!

...The weather must have been better in those days because they could be hung out could your clothes and when we came back in at teatime they were dry enough for ironing...

**How did you air them?**

Oh just on clothes-horses or on a rail over your fireplace. When babies were there, that's where all your nappies went to air, either over the rail over your fireplace or on the large fireguard. In those days, of course, you didn't have airing cupboards or tanks or anything - I mean there was no hot water by tap, everything had to be boiled. Some people had pulleys - I had one up here when I first came - pulleys that you let up and down; in fact I think next door still have one because I can hear it going up and down at times.

**Mr Thomas also remembers the copper his mother used.**

...There was a copper, for washing days, with a hole up in the roof for the steam to go out. The copper was heated from a small fire underneath, and you had to have a little shovel and keep throwing coal in to get the heat going. That was eventually taken out and they got a gas copper. Mother did get a gas oven put in the kitchen, and she had a new range put in which wasn't recognisable; a lot of the features of the old one had vanished - I mean the little tank of water and that kind of thing. But there was no need for that tank of water, really, because you had a tap in the kitchen and, although it was a cold one, it was alright. She also had a gas pipe running round, I remember, at the back of the kitchen table under the window; there was a little nozzle on it, and you could put a flexible tube on it, and she used to put that on to a gas iron. She also had flat-irons which went on to the fire bar.

**Miss Prentice**

The cottage I lived in had a shed at each side of the yard; one side had a copper in it for boiling clothes and they did their washing in it; in the other side we had our dustbins...

**Did you share the copper with other people?**

Oh yes, with four houses; those who'd been there longest got first choice and we used to agree amongst ourselves who used it. I know mother used to do it mainly on a Monday, and [one of the two] ladies on the bottom of the yard had a biggish family and she used to do a bit of washing each day. It was quite a big yard so if you put a big clothes-line out it could hold quite a few things...

**Can you remember much about the ritual of washday?**

Oh, mother used to have a peggy: she had a wooden one, and a wooden handle with a round stool with four or six little legs to it and a handle to the tap - you just started to swish round and round. Later, of course, she had a zinc tub and a posser; it had a suction sort of thing with holes at the side and when you put it down the water seemed to go through it and the suction up and down used to fetch dirt out... For anything that was really dirty she had a rubbing-board and a bit of soap, and she soaked

Washing was very hard work. Even when washing machines became available most people could not afford them, so for much of the twentieth century, the dolly-peg, posser, and dolly-tub were standard equipment. (Courtesy of York Castle Museum.)

them and gave them a bit of a rubbing. And then, of course, they used to see that they'd got all the dirty marks out and put 'em through the wringer, and give them a couple of rinses - the last was with Reckitt's Blue...

**Mr Armstrong describes a similar process.**

The kitchen had a sink, gas oven, and a copper for heating the water on washday. This was always on a Monday when the copper was filled with water and the fire was lit and the water allowed to boil. The peggy-tub was a wooden one; hot water was put in and the clothes had to soak...and then they were churned about with the peggy-stick. [The peggy-stick] was like a small four-leg stool with a wooden post about three foot long fitted to the centre and a handle at the top which was turned back and forth in a twisting motion. The clothes were then taken from the tub and scrubbed on a table with brush and soap. The tub was emptied and refilled again with clean water and the clothes were rinsed. The next stage was to put the washing through the wringing machine - this was also called a mangle - and the two wooden rollers squeezed the water out and back into the tub.

**Mrs Thomlinson recalls her mother's hard work but does not remember washday with affection.**
On Saturday she used to have to wash outside in the copper in the yard; we had a yard and a shed and an outside toilet - oh I hated those Saturday mornings. I think we always detested washday, it did used to be so cold. But golly she was a lovely washer; I still have some sheets - she's been dead about thirteen years now - and you can tell her sheets are white to mine. Yes, she was a marvellous washer; well, they did it all in stages, didn't they? They boiled and rinsed, then rinsed in blue and starched. Oh, if you open the draw you can see her sheets are white to mine after all these years. I don't use them very often because I think they look so nice; I just keep them for when visitors come.
[It was] really hard work, you know. Mind, the steam was outside; you didn't get it in the house because our copper was absolutely out in the yard - no cover over or anything. It always had to be done on a Saturday because she was back on Monday... She put water in the [tub] and really got at it with a peggy-stick.

**And then did she put the washing back in the copper?**
Yes, she'd lift it in and out with a copper-stick, and the copper-stick was what went in the top of the peggy-stick. She used to take that out and lift the washing in and out with it - really hard work. When I had children me mother used to come up on a Monday to wash for me; she still loved washing although she'd had it hard all her life. She was proud of her washing: when you had a yard and your washing hung up you could be very proud then in your own little life.

**How did you manage in the winter for drying clothes?**
Well, sometimes on a wet day I can remember coming in from school and the place was full - a line down the kitchen, a clothes-horse round the fire, oh golly... Then they'd iron 'cause me mother always had it to do at night when she came home; so we hadn't much life really because she was always working. After she'd washed her clothes...she didn't always dry them real, she just left them a little bit damp and then used to fold them and put them through the wringer again [to semi-iron them].

**Mrs Armstrong's mother had one of the early washing machines.**
The houses have now been pulled down, of course, and flats built a more modern way. Mother had a washing machine which was reasonably modern; it had a mangle, you know, and it was the posser type you moved backwards and forwards. And she had an electric boiler - you see, you always used to boil whites in that day, they didn't have these magic powders they have today that makes whites whiter than white, they just had to boil anyway with stains, you know. You used to rent [boilers] at one time - same as the immersion heater - you paid so much a quarter. Anyway, she had

this electric boiler and after a few years they said, "You can keep the boiler," but they forgot to take it off the account and she was still paying for it.

**Mrs Rennison explains the change from using a copper in the early 1950's to having her first washing machine.**

When we moved in here there was a gas copper - a free standing thing - and I had a peggy-tub and a posser, and a small rubber rollered [machine] on a stand. You put your tub under the stand and washed like that. I can remember the day I went into labour with David, I was actually putting the washing in and possing and I had to put it to one side. You used to put your whites in first and poss [them] and then they used to go into your copper. Of course, your first lot of water was heated in your copper to put into your wash-tub.

**How did you get the water out of the copper?**

Oh, it had a tap low down and you had to bucket the stuff out and you carried it across to your peggy-tub. When you got [the clothes] through the soapy water you used to empty your peggy-tub and refill with your clean water to start again so it was quite a lengthy business. I think it used to take me nearly all day when the boys were small.

I think it would be about '59 when I got me first washer, and I went through one thing to another; I went to an Empress, a Hotpoint Empress which was about the biggest machine you could buy. It had the rubber rollers and they were automatic so that was great, you know: you didn't have to turn like you did with the old other one that I had. Again you used to have to lift your washing out with your tongs because it was so hot, and put it through the thing and into your drainer or sink or whatever. Then again, if you wanted to rinse you had to empty your washer and then refill with your clean water so it was still [time consuming]. At least you didn't have to be possing; it took all that work out of it for you and, of course, the turning of the mangle... You were getting somewhere then. [It used] to heat as well - plug that in and fill it up and it used to heat; I used to fill it with quite a bit of warm water then it didn't take quite as long. That was my first washing machine.

**Mrs Thomlinson also welcomed the new washing machines.**

[I got my first electric washing machine] about thirty-six years ago - I'd just had my second baby. The first washers were called Ada washers and they were upright with a roller and they used to put the washing in and then put it through the rollers by electric over the sink. They had a pipe from the tub that emptied but then you'd got to change the water yourself to rinse. The big thing was - oh, you could bring them to boiling point - but you got this lovely electric roller took out all the wringing, you

An advertisement for one of the early washing machines. The Horton Electric Washer was still expensive at £17.17.0 in 1938. (Courtesy of York Castle Museum.)

see. After I'd had that about a year or so the twin-tub came out; they washed one side and then you had to lift them out into the other. I think people still use those. The next stage I got - a great ambition - to have a front loader, and that's what I worked up to; it would have been ten years before I reached that stage.

Once you got these rollers they wrung your clothes out a lot drier than the ordinary wringer machine. And then the spin driers took away the steam from the house, and I haven't reached the tumble drier stage. But you don't get...well, we used to have clothes hanging around on clothes-horses for a full day drying, but the electricity certainly got a lot more water out of them. Washday's nothing now is it? Whereas you dreaded it, absolutely dreaded the thought of washing and then washing your floor afterwards [because] you'd water all over with lifting your clothes in and out. Now with this front loader it's absolutely marvellous.

**Mrs Graham explains how ironing was done before modern technology.**

Well, we had one of those flat-irons and a piece of emery paper...because it got sooted and dirted... Every time you ironed you cleaned it with this emery board and, of course, you had a shuttle service backwards and forwards, one hotting while the other [was being used]...

**And how did you know whether you'd got the right temperature?**

That was the professional part about it: you spat on it to know if it was ready. It's something that comes with use; we had those knitted squares, you know, that you put over the handle, and then you just tested it.

**Did you ever burn anything?**

No, not a lot, but things were apt to get dirty - you perhaps hadn't got a wee bit of soot off... I don't think you burnt them as readily as you would with an electric iron, but you often got smut that moved about... It was hard work; we'd all those frills and the Lord knows what, wasn't there, to iron? Oh dear! And lots of pin-tucks. Blouses were lovely and they were all in cotton; you never let them get too dry on the line; you took them in and you had a squirter thing, like an orange, and you did this with it, then rolled them up. You didn't iron them the same day, they had to lay. Something in that: if they rolled them up, you know, if they rolled up a shirt and put the sleeves over, next day it would iron really lovely - I still do that. Old nighties were all pin-tucks and oh, the christening gown, oh dear: all that embroidery anglaise work, every bit. Lace curtains, they had to starch those and they were all scalloped edged, and they had to pummel these until they were right. Some of the gooey starch got stuck, you know...

**How did you actually starch them?**

Well, you mix this starch - Coleman's Starch - it's like white powder, and you get a blue bag and put that in, and then you pour boiling water 'till it changes from an opaque sort of look to clear. You stir it all the time and then it's ready, but I've done many, many a thing which stood up with itself because it got too much in!

**Mrs Rennison remembers the change from flat-irons to electric ones.**

...Mum had an electric iron before I left home and since I was married we never used flat-irons - that was more when I was a child really. There again, [electric irons] have improved such a lot, haven't they? There's the one that just heated, now it's steam and all these other things. And, of course, using an electric iron, as opposed to the flat-irons, was much better and quicker 'cause you weren't heating them up all the time on the fire or gas; and they kept constant heat, whereas you start getting cold and you had to swap. You usually had two flat-irons so that was a bit time consuming as well, you know.

**Mrs Thomlinson was similarly pleased with the new irons.**

...That's hard work gone, you see. I mean, we used to have to rub soap on the flat-iron just to keep it clean; then we did away with the fire because we used to put them near the fire to heat... Mind, they didn't have ironing boards when I was first married, they just used to do them on the kitchen table on the blanket. I don't know how we managed... I was very thrilled when I got it.

A selection of irons ranging from the simple flat-iron to an early electric model. Electric irons were one of the first truly popular electric appliances. (Courtesy of York Castle Museum.)

# HOUSEHOLD CLEANING

Even with modern equipment keeping a house clean involves continual work. This chapter illustrates how the work and the attitudes towards it have changed.

**Mrs Rennison**

...Most people's houses were very clean. They were always scrubbing their doorsteps and everything, you know; it was something that seemed to be done so regularly, probably every day. Even if it wasn't scrubbed it was washed, and they used to wash sort of a half-moon outside and then the steps were done with a 'step-stone' all along the edges; you could have eaten off doorsteps. A 'step-stone' was a bit like pumice really, but it was a creamy colour and you used to scrub your steps and then finish it at the side. You used to rub the edge...and it gave like a sandy colour, and sometimes they did a fancy pattern... They took a pride in their houses although they were only small, and it must have been hard because, you know yourself, if you've got a lot of clutter in a room it's harder to do than if it's a big room with two or three things in. They were only very small houses with small rooms and yet every day they were dusted. I mean now I don't dust sometimes for a week or a fortnight but they did it every day, religiously dusted and cleaned cupboards out...and the windows, putting clean curtains up. I've told me mother when she's talked about me front sometimes, I've said, "Mother, I live inside. I don't live on the front." I'm not bothered about the outside but every day they used to sweep their fronts... You don't get all the smuts they used to get. When they'd just done the front and the clean window-sill, if there were any smuts, oh they'd go mad wouldn't they? They'd be out again with cloth cleaning it all off.

**Mrs Moore was asked if her daughters helped her in the house.**

Oh yes, at cleaning time and always on Friday. You were never done when you'd washing, ironing, and bedrooms to do - there were three bedrooms with two beds in each room. You were forced to do so much on a night, you see, if he [Mr Moore] was on nights and in bed during the day. It had to be done at weekends so one of them had to do it; it didn't matter which one's turn it was, if it was their week they had to stop and give me a hand no matter how much they wanted to go out. I've come in many a time Friday night and I've been rushing around trying to get scrubbed through the kitchen. I don't know but Friday was an awful day for me:

he was maybe getting up, and our Eddy would be getting up, and either one or the other would be wanting dinner. You can't work and cook dinner, can you? At least I couldn't. And babies to see to - I don't know how I did it but I did - and they used to say, "Oh, I'm sick of seeing you with that floor-cloth in your hand, we'll get you a mop." We got a mop and I didn't like it because it didn't get in the corners. "Oh, it's no good to me," I said. "You can use it when you do the floor." And we went on like that because my kitchen had the dining room off, and there was a front room. It was a good family house because they could go in the front room to do their homework; even when they got to High School they used to go in there and it still left us the dining room. It was very small but comfy... I don't know how I got through the work sometimes, I often wonder...

**Did the girls have special jobs?**

Well no, but they took it in their turn. One of them perhaps had some classes, or if they'd arranged to go out anywhere, well the other one would take over that week... They always ironed their own things, that was the rule; I washed but they ironed their own. [They'd rush] out sometimes when they wanted to go to a dance; our Myra went to lots of dances and I've heard her say to our Joyce, "Can you finish them? I must go..." She used to go with a girl from work, Sheila, and sometimes she'd be late meeting her. They used to swap round but I never had quarrelling and they knew what they had to do and they got on and did it.

**Mr Pilgrim remembers how his sister was also expected to help their mother with the housework.**

My sister did the baking at the weekend but I think it was because mother was trying to teach her to do the domestic chores. That was expected of a girl in those days: you know, to teach them how to cook and whatnot, and eventually how to wash. She used to make the beds with mother's help, and I suppose during the week they did a bit of a clean through the house; but I know that at weekends everywhere was scrubbed through clean, right from the back to the front, donkey-stoning the step etc, and even swilling the little pavement flags in front of your house.

**Mrs Burton helped her mother and describes the ingenious way she cleaned carpets before they had a vacuum cleaner.**

...Wednesday we used to do the bedrooms, turning everything out properly - of course we'd no hoovers or anything. You had a long brush, you see, a stiff brush but a long one. I don't know whether I had... but I know mother had a dustpan on her toe, and you sort of moved about with this thing on your toe and swept the dust into it. Mother always did her carpets like that.

**Miss Kirby went into service at the beginning of the century, well before vacuum cleaners were widely available.**

I went to where my sister lived. I went as a between-maid, it's a horrible job. You work with the parlour-maid first thing in the morning from half-past six 'till breakfast time; after breakfast you work with the house-maid 'till lunchtime; after lunch you work in the kitchen with the cook. You'd never a dull moment; never a slack moment either! [To do the cleaning] you had a dustpan, a long sweeping-brush, and two hand brushes - a soft one and a stiff one. You just got down on your hands and knees and brushed. I had a girl come here once to help me as a home-help and she didn't know how to hold a sweeping brush; she'd push and push and push, and she shoved everything under the carpet. She didn't sweep it up; she had nothing at the end. Well, I could always produce a full dustpan...

**Miss Kirby and Mrs Moore describe how dishes were cleaned before washing-up liquid.**

[Before washing-up liquid] soda was used but, you see, you got very sore hands, they got chapped... There was some very nice green cleaning soap called Watson's, and there was Lifebuoy - there still is Lifebuoy - and Sunlight. You didn't have to leave the piece of soap in the water or else you might feel a smack on your back for doing it. They'd rub some soap on a dishcloth to make the water soapy, and then wash up like that.

'The Romantic Image'. A Sunlight Soap advertisement c.1910. (Courtesy of York Castle Museum.)

### Mrs Moore

We used soda if it was very greasy, common washing soda. There was only one washing powder - I've seen it in the museum in little packets - did they call it Hudson's? That was the only washing powder I can remember but we never used it because me mother said it was too expensive. Soda was cheaper; you only needed a little bit in to soften your water if it were greasy and we'd plenty of hot water.

### Miss Kirby was asked if cleaning the grates took a long time.

Oh yes. Well, you see, you used to buy black lead in a little wrapper, it was nearly like a sausage. It was in some sort of greaseproof paper and you used to tip that piece of black lead into a little black lead pot; and you had a little round brush and you put a drop of water on it, and then you put that on... You had black lead brushes and you polished it off; it took a lot of doing really, a lot of brushing. The thing was you didn't want to make it too wet, and yet if you didn't make it wet enough you got too much black lead into the brush and then you got into trouble.

### Mr Armstrong describes his living room and the black leading involved in keeping it clean.

The living room had a cooking range with an oven on the left of the fire and a water heater on the right; there was a 'tidy betty' to keep the hot ashes from falling onto the hearth. The range and 'tidy betty' were black leaded and polished each week; this consisted of putting the black lead mixture on with a damp cloth and then being polished with a brush and duster. The handles of the oven and the hinge bars were bright steel and were cleaned with emery paper to shine them up. The tap on the water container was brass polished, and the hearth was whitened with 'Hearth's Heart Stone' which was mixed in a saucer and rubbed on with a wet cloth and left to dry. Standing in the hearth was a fender with fire-irons consisting of tongs, poker, rake, and shovel; these were also steel and kept bright and shiny with emery paper. Over the fire was a bar and a hook to hang the kettle off. The range was really highly polished with this black lead...and, oh, it absolutely shone. They were very proud of their kitchens - well, their living rooms - in those days.

### Like others, Mr Armstrong was expected to help around the house.

We all had our jobs... One of us had to clean the shoes and boots - every night they were always cleaned and polished. When my father came home his boots were quite muddy but they had to be cleaned that night before he went to work the following morning. He wouldn't go to work with dirty boots.

The Albert Kitchener, a range made by the firm of Thomlinson Walker of Walmgate, York, from the mid-1860's. (Courtesy of York Castle Museum.)

**Was there a different selection of things the girls had to do?**

The girls used to have to help with the washing-up and sometimes had to wash the floors - the floors were washed about every other day. There was no carpets such as we know them, there was just those hand-pricked rugs about the floor. The floors were those red-stone tiles but they didn't polish them - not in the living room and kitchen - they just scrubbed them and washed them.

**Mrs Armstrong's neighbours had large families and she remembers that the children had to work hard.**

We were surrounded by large families. Next door through the garage, he was Chief Engineer, and there were seven in that family. Our other friends, the other side of the road, their father was a chef on the trains and there were six; so I had plenty of playmates, there was no problem, but they all had to do duties about the house because, with being big families, the older ones had to look after the younger ones and so on, and do the household jobs as well.

**She also describes how the bedrooms had to be cleaned.**

Wednesday was the day the bedrooms were cleaned thoroughly - everything 'bottomed' as they called it - everything brought out of its place and back. The floors, of course, were lino with rugs at the side - no carpets. The press had to be kept clean and the floors were sort of wiped over with a damp cloth rather than a duster; it collected the dust up better. There were no machines, no hoovers or anything like that. All the ornaments had to be dusted and everything - it really was the big day for the bedrooms.

...When we'd finished all our work we had spring cleaning in March and April, and what an upheaval that was. Every room had to be sorted out again; even if it had only been done the week before. Curtains had to be washed - and net curtains. Did you used to pull yours into shape? We used to like that little bit, standing at the end and pulling them so they were straight. You couldn't iron them, you see; we just hung them straight up again. That was mostly part of spring cleaning - that and decorating. Goodness, what a time it was! [Decorating] was paper mostly; it was taken off every two years and new put up. Ceilings were done with lime - whitewash - what they called limewash. The next thing that came was 'Wall Pamur': that was like a thick white liquid. I wondered that, 'mur' is French for 'wall', isn't it? 'Mur', that's how it came to be put on the wall. The lime was very bad: it used to spoil any other decor, it had to be washed right off. When it came on to the other stuff it used to burn straight through. But we had a lot of dark colours; the green was very popular in our house. Do you remember the wall paper for halls called 'Lincrusta'? That was dark, very thick paper with a gloss on it so when you came through the door and rubbed on it you didn't make it dirty because it could be washed off. And it was very tough as well in case you knocked it with anything in the halls. You see, most things had to come down through the halls, anything to be moved or anything like that, and halls were very narrow.

**Mrs Rennison also remembers spring cleaning and explains the difference made by the vacuum cleaner.**

[My mother's first vacuum cleaner] was a Ewbank cylinder vacuum, and then when I got married and moved here there was an old vac left in the house; again it was a Ewbank but it was one of the upright type. Oh, it was a horrible thing really 'cause it had no tools or anything with it. You could just go over the carpets with it [but] there were no tools that you could do the stairs with so, of course, you still used your small brush and dust-pan. In those days we didn't have fitted carpets because there were just carpet squares with the wood surround downstairs, and upstairs in the bedrooms we had linoleum down and just rugs so you were able to sweep those with the sweeping brush and wash them over each week. And then, I think it was a Hoover that I bought for myself but at the same time I used a Ewbank carpet sweeper... I used both and I found that that

An advertisement for Eureka Vacuum Cleaners. Cussins and Light imported high quality appliances from the United States in the 1930's. (Courtesy of York Castle Museum.)

was quite useful when the children were small. Just getting up crumbs, getting the carpet sweeper out instead of the vacuum cleaner out.

**Do you remember your mother buying that first vacuum cleaner?**

Yes, she was quite excited by it. I suppose now, when you think about it, we've not had to wait 'till we're as old as they were. What would she be? Probably early forties before she ever had an electric vacuum.

**Was she happy with it - did she feel it did the job as well?**

Oh yes, there again I think it must be just the way they were brought up that you still did the spring cleaning. Today we don't seem to make such a big issue of it because we're able to hoover each week, and even able to do the picture moulds each week because we've got things we can use. I can remember me mum taking all the carpets up, and out on the lines, and beating them and that. I suppose I did it when I first got married, I can't really remember, but I did have the one vacuum and I did take the carpets up because I can remember cleaning them and hanging them on the line to dry.

**The carpet was actually lifted off the floor?**

Yes, about once a year. So I suppose fitted carpets have made a big difference really... That [first] was an upright cleaner, then I went on to the cylinder type and I've stuck with the cylinder type ever since. The tools are useful, of course, for doing your suites and everything, aren't they? But I know the first one was a real ancient thing.

# COOKING AND BAKING

**With the wide availability of pre-cooked food far less time is now spent on cooking. This chapter recalls the days when most of the cooking and baking were done at home.**

**Mrs Armstrong describes baking day.**

In our house Tuesday was baking day and we spent most of the day - morning anyway - cooking lots of things. Mostly we used to make meat pies to have for lunch and dinner, and then lots of pastry, bread and cakes—always your own bread, never bought. Anyway, that was Tuesday spent up doing the baking.

**Did you always make white bread?**

Yes, always white. Odd times we would make fruit loaves but mostly it was white bread and white bread cakes.

**Did you make tea cakes with fruit in?**

Yes, that's right. We made all the scones [and] plum cakes, then we made them on the shelf.

**Oven bottom cake?**

Yes...and they had a crust, very much like French bread in a way, and lady cakes as well... [We also made] tarts, cream buns, jam buns, lemon curd and Yorkshire curd tart... It was a week's baking.

Usually mother used to [bake] with the help of one of the maids, but after we left the business in 1932 my mother used to do it on her own, of course. We went into a private house in Huntington, she did all the work just the same but on a lesser scale.

**Alternatively, Mrs Rennison's mother baked on Friday.**

You used to come in at lunchtime and see the great big bowls with the dough rising, and when you came in at teatime there was the gorgeous smell of tea and all the teacakes or whatever had been made. That's the one thing me mum did a lot was baking... There again, it was usually all very plain sort of baking - she was never one for making a lot of cakes except at Christmas. She didn't make many buns but she used to do a lot of fruit pies and jam tarts and nearly all pastry baking, you know. Bread and teacakes we used to have as well, so we didn't used to go short that way.

Some examples of cooking equipment, including a multi-purpose pancheon, cast iron saucepans, a pudding boiler and an egg whisk. (Courtesy of York Castle Museum.)

**Mrs Burton describes how they made butter on their farm.**

We didn't get a lot of milk but we didn't go in for selling it, we just had for ourselves. We had a big separator and we used to separate it, and we always kept all the cream and used what we wanted that day, and what was left used to go into the pantry. In a week's time it was full, you see, and I used to churn [and] make perhaps fourteen or twenty pounds of butter.

I never made cheese. Sometimes you would be half a day getting the butter: it would what we call 'go to sleep' and you weren't turning the cream round, and you'd be churning perhaps an hour and the wretched stuff wasn't doing any good. It was a whole half-day's work, churning... You could hear it turning [and] when it didn't we called it 'going to sleep'. When it waked up you could hear the cream going round, you see, and you could tell by the turning... It was a very big churn we had, a very big churn; it could have taken, I should think, thirty pounds or perhaps forty pounds, if you'd had it. We never had as much as that but it was a huge churn. You used to churn and then you rinsed the butter - there was just a plug at the bottom where you let the water out. We used to put two or three lots of cold water on when it came to butter, you see, and then we turned it 'till it all got into a solid mass, not little bits - into a whole piece. Then we used to wash it two or three times with cold water, and salt it, and then work it in the churn with your hands. Then I used to make it into pounds with my two hands and we used to mark it - we had a fancy thing you just ran on, a flower or something, a little wheel that went round. I don't think you'd see them, I don't think you'd find one now. Well you wouldn't because nobody makes butter now, do they?

**Mrs Hadley still makes her own lemonade.**

My mother and father didn't like me having fizzy lemonade, we had our own lemonade; but 'pop' we were more excited to have because it was something we didn't have at home. You know what children are, always wanting something... I still make my own lemonade, I have it every day. I squeeze the lemons first of all and put them in a jug, then I cut the rind up and put that in, then I put boiling water on, then even for my own children in the summer I used to put in cream of tartar. My own children only had 'pop' on Christmas or birthdays because I think the other is better for them. You see, people couldn't afford to buy shop things, that's why they made so much of their own. It was an extravagance, wasn't it, until it came to the later years? I wasn't keen on it anyway, it was a novelty, something different.

**She also remembers the types of food her family ate when she was a child.**

Grown ups had egg and bacon for breakfast but we young ones didn't - I didn't anyway. We had just porridge and/or bread and dripping. I can't think of any egg and bacon 'till we were older. Then lunchtime was ordinary Yorkshire pudding, we used to have those quite regularly... We didn't used to have dinners like they do now; the midday meal was always dinner and then tea at teatime. We had a roast of some sort and at the weekend it was usually beef. You didn't have much soup, did you? Now we have soup and something else but then it was usually straight into your Yorkshire pud, or sago, or apple tart and custard, something like that. At teatime the man of the house was the main person, he had the best things.

**Mrs Armstrong and Mrs Hadley discuss the preparation of food before frozen produce became available.**

**Mrs Armstrong**

Anything like onions or anything else - veg - was chopped up on a board. My grandad used to be able to do beans beautiful, lovely slices of runner beans. Anything you did you did yourself, there was nothing bought or prepared, was there? No frozen food at all, you went and bought the fresh stuff and sorted it out. I think [we were] used to growing our own food and everything being fresh; my husband doesn't like frozen food at all, and he doesn't like tinned food either, so we get fresh at this time of year.

**Did you have tinned food?**

**Mrs Hadley**

Tinned salmon was the main, and tinned fruit, that's all as I remember. Tinned salmon was a favourite - simply gorgeous at teatimes. John West, I think that was the only one.

**Were tinned foods considered a treat?**

Yes, tinned salmon and tinned pears rather than fresh fruit - we nearly always had fresh fruit.

**Mrs Armstrong particularly remembers the traditional food on a Sunday.**

It was the day of the week we usually had roast beef and Yorkshire pudding; well, I should say it was the other way round because you had Yorkshire pudding with gravy first, then meat and potatoes [with] veg, [followed by] apple pie with custard.

**Mr Pilgrim recalls that he was luckier than many to have a Sunday meal.**

Oh yes, Sunday dinner was the dinner of the week: it was quite a special thing. We had mashed and roast potatoes, vegetables and a piece of meat; and very few people did, quite frankly, have a joint of meat. A joint of meat when I were getting them were from two to three shillings a joint. I know quite a few households that would probably buy a rabbit at ninepence or tenpence, or a big one for a shilling. But if you had the joint of meat, that was the highlight of the week, that was the great Sunday dinner when you finished with rhubarb pie or apple pie with custard, and Sunday tea. [Sometimes] we sat down to jelly with cream as a sort of extra to the normal Sunday tea which was home-made cakes or home-made scones, and which you particularly had on Sunday rather than any other day of the week. So Sunday was quite an eating day, you know, when everyone gathered in their best suits and clean shirts; it was the day when everybody dressed up in their best clobber and presented themselves round the table.

**Mrs Rennison's Sunday tea was slightly different.**

Sunday tea was stewed prunes and I can remember she [Mrs Rennison's mother] used to soak them overnight and they were all wrinkled; and as a special treat you'd have sliced lemon in these prunes, and custard. Yes, that was your Sunday tea and that was great... When eventually you could get fruit again - bananas and that - after the war, that was your treat on a Sunday: fruit and custard with your tea.

**Mrs Armstrong**

Teatime, of course, was usually boiled ham or tinned salmon - that was a favourite - and pastries and cakes that mother baked. Suppertime we usually just had a drink of milk or Allenbury's Food which was like Cow and Gate: you mix it up with water, put your milk in, and when we had that we went to bed on it - no meal at night. That was really all we had.

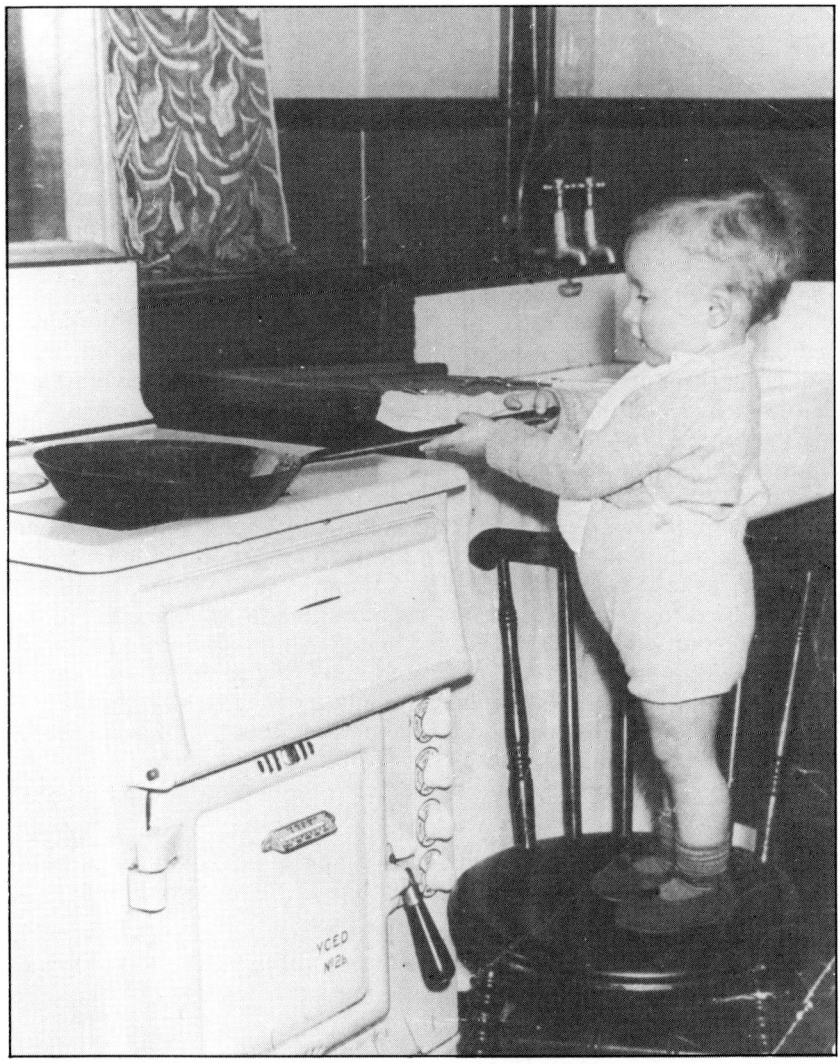

**This cooker was rented from York City Electrical Department. Renting appliances from gas and electrical companies was common in the 1920's and 1930's. (Courtesy of Yorkshire Evening Press.)**

# WOMEN WORKING

The preceding chapters describe work done in the home, but many women needed an income and they often found themselves doing similar work for other people.

**Miss Prentice was in service and lived in.**

Well, I would get up about seven and get washed - we had a basin, you see - get washed and dressed. I'd go downstairs and first of all I'd do the servants' fireplace, and Fanny'd be down and she'd make a pot of tea and we'd have a cup of tea each, then she used to go back and do some bedrooms upstairs and I used to go up and do their dining room fires. [I'd] clean them up, and there was a second and there was some brass on that as well; I had to rake them out, cinders and everything. I had this special wooden box and it had a shelf and I had this little hand brush and I put cinders in the bottom and then put me shelf back. There used to be another man come - he sort of swept up outside passage and everything, like a roadman - and he used to come and fill coal buckets for us. [After that] I'd come down and lay breakfast for us and I used to get things ready for butler to take up breakfast upstairs. Fanny used to come down and then we used to clear all breakfast pots away, wash 'em up, and I used to clean up our servants' carpets; I had one of them push-horns and I used to sweep along with that, and dust, and make our room alright. Fanny would be doing our bedrooms and bathroom...and then we started planning for dinner. I'd peel potatoes and whatever vegetables there was to put to boil - they weren't cooked with us not having a cook often on a Sunday or Saturday; she'd cook a big joint of beef or whatever and we used to serve that up.

**Miss Worfolk's mother had a draper's shop and so the family had a maid to look after the house. She remembers one of the girls very well.**

I was about ten when we got the first girl living in, but the one I remember particularly was this girl who came from an orphanage; she came and mother had to teach her everything, she knew nothing. One of the early days mother took some celery through for her to do for tea and, of course, mother was busy in the shop so she just left the girl... [When she] went through for tea there was all the outside of the celery in the vase. Mother said, "Where is the inside, Elsie, the heart of the celery?" "Oh," she said, "I wrapped that up in newspaper and put it in the dustbin." "What?" said

Four women who worked as domestic cleaners in York. (Courtesy of Mrs Mennell.)

mother, "That is the part we eat! The outside we might eat for a vegetable." "In the home we never saw that." The staff got it, the little kids got the outside... They can't have taught the poor girl much.

**Could you describe a typical day for the maid?**

My father had to be at work by half past seven, I used to get up at half past six, so I imagine she would get up about then, get the fire and get his breakfast, and probably mother and I would go down a bit later, and she would get our breakfast. Then, of course, I would go off to school and mother would go into the shop, and Elsie would be left to clean up, bring coal in, wash windows, everything that has to be done in the house, under supervision at first.

**Would she have time off in the week?**

Oh yes, she was given quite a bit of time off. In fact, as I said, she had every night if she wanted it, to go out, and she'd to be in by ten, but Saturday nights nine... She had her own bedroom but she used to sit with us at night, but she wasn't often in. I think she used to go to the boy's home, he lived not far away.

**Mrs Moore's mother also ran a shop and they did the baking for their customers.**

I used to have a stool and me dad cut a rib out so as the bowl dropped in and it was fastened on this... I don't know if you remember those big zinc bowls with handles at each end. [My mother] was only little and she couldn't even use a chair to kneel on to knead. Well, she used to lay a stone of flour in bread at night before she went to bed at eleven, and get up next morning - she was never in bed after about seven - and that was baked for breadcakes for breakfast. And whilst she was waiting she used to be making teacakes up to rise ready to go in when the bread finished, she had a proper method like that. That was for sale in the shop and they used to make Christmas cakes. Me father and me used to have to clean all the fruit; we used to shake it in a pillow case - I wonder what they do now? - and cut the peel up that was all shaped. We took orders for cakes... We had to weigh up then in the shop, you know, and when stuff came in - it was ordered on the Monday, came in on the Tuesday - me mother weighed it all herself on her own scales and tipped it on to squares of paper. We taught me dad how to wrap it up - and twist the bottom in, you know - by half pounds and pounds. It was blue paper for granulated sugar and fine sugar was in red - there was all sorts of sugar.

**Mrs Thomlinson worked in a cafe.**

My friend asked me to go and work at this cafe and I daren't tell me mother, so I went and worked one day on the Saturday to see if I liked it. I knew that would be it if I took a job...'cause me mother would lose five shillings and that would be dreadful. Anyhow, I went to work at this cafe and it was hard work. I got eight and fivepence a week for about sixty hours and if you worked over you got a half day off when they were quiet, you'd no overtime. But I must have liked it 'cause I stuck it; I suppose work was bad then really - that would be in about the thirties. I think I left or got sacked about four times and I still went back. After I'd been there about a year me mother said, "You must ask for a rise." I said, "I don't think I dare," and she said, "You must." So I asked for a rise and on the Friday night he assembled all the waitresses, all the shop staff - I was just like kitchen staff, really the lowest paid I suppose - and I stood there and he said to them all, "This girl has asked me for a rise." Well I said, "My mother said I had to do it," and he said, "Don't ever do that again. I'll give you one this time." Well what an embarrassment... I got ten and fivepence so I got a two shilling rise, but I never did ask for another one - I knew it was more than my life was worth! Well, I worked there 'till I was about twenty and I finished up in charge of the bakehouse. I got moved to the bakehouse for chattering but I liked the work. I was getting about two or three pounds a week which was a lot of money then, and they said they could get a man for that to do night work...

**Mrs Burton remembers Emma Johnson, a woman who worked for their family.**

She hadn't anything, she just had an old mother live with her in this little cottage. She used to go and set potatoes at Newton, and then walk home to Wilberfoss to dress her mother's foot, and then go back to work again. And when she had the baby she just went home from setting potatoes, had the baby, and went back to work the same afternoon... I'd three children and four men - my husband and farmhands - in the household and Emma did everything for them: cooked and set the meals, washed up, made the beds every morning, scrubbed the staircase - it was a winding staircase - and the bedroom floor; just scrubbed every week - there were no carpets or anything, just very sparse. She worked from morning 'till night. Every evening she used to get the axe and fill up with kindling, and go out and fill with logs ready for morning, because she had to have the fire burning and the kettle boiling at six o'clock, you see, which was a big thing in those days. We hadn't any electricity for many years after I went to Wilberfoss... Well, she did nothing but work; she'd no pleasure in this life - just worked up to her death. If anyone was ill she used to sit up all the night 'till the doctor came. She wouldn't go to bed if any of the children were ill; she used to sit up knitting socks - she was always knitting socks for her son.

She used to go and get washed about three o'clock; she used to take the boiler tin, dip it in the boiler at the side of the fire, and go through the room from the kitchen to get upstairs - I always saw her going then. She always got washed about three o'clock, and then she used to sit and knit socks 'till teatime at five o'clock, and the men had the meal at six. It was very hard work, though... She used to go to everything; if anything went wrong on any of the farms they used to fetch Emma. Whatever calamity there was they used to fetch Emma. That was funny that, wasn't it?

When my husband started with pneumonia, Dr Isherwood - he was our doctor from Pocklington all our life - he said, "You ought to have a fire." So I said, "Oh well, I'll put a fire on." He said, "I'll go down and get some sticks and I'll light the fire." So he went down to the kitchen, and when he came back he said, "It's like getting gold, getting a dry stick from Emma!" I said, "Well, if you had to have a big kettle boiling at six o'clock, you wouldn't be so keen if you'd bothered to chop it to size!" But it's unthinkable now, isn't it?

# SHOPPING AND HOUSEHOLD ECONOMY

**This chapter recalls the days before large supermarkets and chain stores when York Market dominated the town centre and corner shops prospered. It also recaptures the austerity of the depression and the war years when many families suffered severe financial hardship.**

**Mrs Rennison**

On a Saturday at Wright's Pork Butchers in Nunnery Lane we used to have to go and queue. There were certain times when the van arrived: it was the ten o'clock van or the two o'clock van and you used to go about an hour before and stand in a queue. When the van arrived the chap would get out with his tray and carry it through on his head, and suddenly there would be a whisper all round the queue, "He's brought some pies, he's bought some pies." You thought, "Oh great, now me mum said if he has any sausage rolls or if he has a pork pie you must get this," but by the time you got to the counter you'd seen the last pie had gone. "Oh what have we got to get now? Will it be poloni or sausage or a bit of brawn?" It was quite funny, I suppose, looking back, but it wasn't in those days because you sort of thought, "Ooh great, we can have sausage rolls today," and by the time you got to the counter the last ones had gone in front of you; if you wanted some you had to wait for the next van which was probably another four hours - you'd to come back again.

We had a little shop at the top of the street that sold groceries and we used to get our bread and everything - you could go up daily for that. [Some people] had stuff on the slate but I can honestly say that my mum would never do that simply because my father was out of work quite a bit and she always maintained that if you couldn't pay that day you couldn't pay the next. Although we had very little money I wouldn't say we were deprived; we didn't perhaps have the things that our kids have today. I mean, I remember once going for a bottle of brown sauce - and that was a luxury - and I can remember dropping it and I really didn't half get into trouble: we'd probably not had a bottle of brown sauce for weeks. I remember hiding under the table because I was terrified I was going to get a good hiding. As I say, you hadn't the money but I don't think we were ever deprived; we always had fruit and things that were necessary... Sweets were all rationed anyway in the war, but this would have

A typical York corner shop with several advertisements for domestic products. (Courtesy of York Environmental Health Department.)

been before the war I would think for I was quite young. I can remember when we were at Mill Mount [School], only in the first year, and we were going to make soap and we had to take fat. She nearly hit the roof, she said, "Fat, you can't take fat for to be making soap; we haven't got enough fat for what we want." I had to take margarine or something, I can't remember what it was we had to take, but oh dear!.. I can remember twenty years ago when me mother moved from Drake Street into a flat, she had pans of soap in a box. She had Oxydol - do you remember that soap powder, Oxydol? - and things like that she had stacked away. I don't suppose they were any good but she'd stored the stuff for years. They'd never throw anything out, would they, in those days? You couldn't afford to waste, even your little bits of soap you used to stick in your copper or a soap saver. Oh I've seen me mother scrape bits of soap into the copper just for extra lather, I suppose soap powder was rationed.

**Mrs Moore remembers the first cut-price stores and York Market at its busiest.**

When they opened that big 'cut' shop in Bootham I went there because we hadn't any shops in Marygate, you see; but there always had to be someone there to meet me because I couldn't lump two big bags. Well,

The twentieth century has seen the rapid growth of national brands. Some of the products shown here are still available while others have disappeared. (Courtesy of York Castle Museum.)

when that came I used to go there, but more often than not, when the children were little, I had a niece who was very good to me - she worked at Terry's - and she would come quite a lot. I had one pram for two with a seat up front, you know, and you couldn't get much underneath, but we used to go to the first 'cut' shop that ever opened, in Church Street. I used to go there because there was coppers off everything: flour was cheaper there than anywhere. It was only a little shop but it was the only one in York at the time. This niece of mine always used to meet me and she would carry so much and I would carry... I always used to get for the week, I was never one to shop every day.

We generally had a walk round the market on Saturday night. If he [Mr Moore] had worked late I would meet him and he'd have a walk round the market with me to see what they were selling off, you know, chickens or ought like that for tea we'd get, or fruit and stuff, and fish. There was one [fishmonger] called 'Wrap it up George' who used to cut a big chunk of a great big fish and then knock it down, such and such, and then shout, 'Wrap it up George!' And you used to get a lovely parcel of fish there which would make our tea and supper as we wanted it. We never went to fish and chip shops, I cooked everything... There was a pot-man used to come,

'Pot Joe', and he used to juggle things: he'd drop them on floor but they never broke. I've loads of things I used to buy - I could have stood there all Saturday watching him. They all had lots of patter that sort, well that was our enjoyment. I never went anywhere.

**Others remember York Market as well.**

**Mrs Armstrong**

We only had the market Saturday. It was in Parliament Street and about half of it was butter women; the other half was fruit and veg, home-made boiled sweets, plants, and a man called 'Wrap it up George' who sold fish. Then there was the pot-man; he used to get all these plates on his arm, throw them up, and catch them - he had right gimmicks. He had a lovely springy board and I remember a big vase - it looked like cut glass but it wouldn't be - and I remember him banging it and it used to bounce a foot high, then he caught it. It was all a gimmick but it was something nice, something interesting. Now they just stand behind the stalls waiting for you to approach them but then they used to draw you with these ideas they made up.

**Mrs Hadley**

We used to go for our butter to the butter market - the farmer's wives used to come in... Where I went to the farm as a girl they used to do the churning and I used to take over from her while she got the men's breakfast ready. Thursday was churning day and the postman who came on Thursday always had a mug of buttermilk. I can remember packing all those half pounds of butter in oblongs; some wanted them in rounds with a swan punched on top. Then the farmer's wife, she used to have a huge basket with spotless starched linen to cover it; she used to take this and go by pony and trap to the main road and then get a bus which went into York for the Saturday. I don't think she stood on the market, she had her regular people she delivered to...

There were market gardeners who came in but that was only Saturdays. It was quite an event to go to market, and later on near closing time they used to sell stock quite cheap - there was no fridges then. You could get lots of oranges for a penny - they wanted to get rid of them, you see, rather than bring them back again.

**Mrs Thomlinson**

The meat market was at this end - St Sampson's Square was all meat. We always went for me grandma's joint...it was always beef, I remember.

**Miss Kirby**

Well, there was about five rows of stalls and it were terrible in the winter

York Market used to fill Parliament Street and St Sampson's Square where this photograph was taken. (Courtesy of Mr C. Minter.)

time. They had covers over, you know, and they sagged a lot; there was a pole in and that was supposed to come over the edge of the stall, but when the wind come - whoop! - and all the water that had drained down into the part that had sagged used to come down. Oh, I've had a bucketful of water down me! You just used to either stand right under the stall or stand well back in the middle of the road and go, "How much are them?" and, "I want that and I want some of those." You either had to do it one way or the other or else you got a ducking.

**Mr Pilgrim shopped for his mother when he was a boy.**

I used to have to go and queue for the groceries at the Co-operative store which was on the corner of Vyner Street and Haxby Road. I suppose I would be somewhere between six and seven, probably nearer seven, because then I would be trusted with probably five bob - you could get an awful lot of little things for five shillings. I well remember that I used to take my sister with me, I suppose to give my mother a chance to get on with the house cleaning... I suppose having to go shopping at an early age I began to know perhaps as much as what a lot of grown-ups did; how much this cost and how much that cost, and how to reckon up the pennies and bring 'em home... I'm certain that we used to buy two pounds of sugar for tuppence ha'penny, and I'm sure that these large bread loaves that we bought for the family were fourpence - I remember there was such an outcry when it went up to fourpence ha'penny, I do remember that. Bacon was somewhere round about a shilling to one and fourpence a pound, and we used to get a pound of jam for fourpence; cakes and tarts that you see in shops now - almost the same really - were a penny. I remember going to Millhouse's, which is another little shop that was on Haxby Road, and getting penny cakes and penny buns. Even Barton's in the city, which was a big shop, used to sell buns at that size with the glazed sugar on top - what they call Bath-buns - they were a penny... Well, I used to go to a butcher in Goodramgate, and this butcher'd been there a long, long time, and I used to go on a Saturday and get quite a big joint of meat for Sunday for two shillings.

**The following passages recall the days of personal service.**

**Mrs Burton**

I used to shop at Grisedale's for my clothes - they were near Woolworth's in Coney Street, nearly opposite Market Street - it was a family concern... It was a very good shop and I preferred it to Rowntree's and Marshall's in those days. It was a personal shop: they sort of knew me and knew what you liked, and they would say to you when you went, "Oh, there's nothing for you today." And if they had anything going cheap they would bring it and say, "This would just suit you." And often you'd buy two things where you'd only buy one.

**Mrs Hadley**

You didn't have supermarkets, did you? You went to the counter and you were attended to, and you had a chair to sit down on.

**Mrs Armstrong**

...There was Coning's in Pavement where the supermarket is now, it sold provisions. Another very good shop was Border's in Coney Street, that was a provision shop that was very popular. Border's used to send round and take your order; later, my mum used to give her order to the man and it was sent round. Most used to [do that] and had a proper delivery service... They used to have the boys on bikes with the big baskets in front delivering as well. Boys from school used to be errand boys, then they would move up to be assistants in the shop, but they nearly all started as errand boys in those big stores. There was no comparison to these big supermarkets; mind, there were a few corner shops you used to go to for odds and ends.

F. T. Burley's greengrocers shop in Micklegate c.1910. (Courtesy of Mr R. H. Burley.)

**Mrs Thomlinson remembers how they got their milk.**

Well, a milkman used to come but we used to slip for half a pint in a jug sometimes from the street nearest if we'd missed the milk, me mother being out. You just couldn't leave it on the doorstep, you see, it was just put in a jug.

**You didn't have it bottled?**

No, we used to have it in a jug [so we] had to be in.

**What about fish and chip shops?**

Oh yes, they were plentiful but it was sort of a bit degrading for me mother to have fish and chips. Of course, I was sent for a bag of chips at night, but I don't think we ever had fish and chips for dinner.

**Mrs Moore introduces the section on household economy.**

We got by but we never had any money to spare to buy anything else. We had the home decently furnished and, of course, I used to make my own covers and cushions; I'd go to the market on Saturday for remnants and make up from there. [The children] never had a bought coat, a frock or anything until they went to Mill Mount [School] and, of course, I couldn't make the uniform then, I had to buy it. I could buy bits and make them blouses and things, but coats, I couldn't make them that; I had to get them and that was the first coat that they ever had bought. I used to wash stuff and press it out and make it up wrong side.

But I never was so poor. We always had good shoes, I was used to it. I always made a practice of buying good shoes and that was the only thing I did at the Co-op. Our Myra had a high instep, Joyce had a long thin foot, they all had different things; I could get our Dorothy with anything on, she always has done. When Co-op started we had a friend came round with what you call a club ticket for weekly payment; it was the only thing I paid weekly, two shillings a week. Then this niece of mine, she married a man who was a shoe-mender at the Co-op. They weren't allowed to do any cobbling on their own at home but he used to do one pair of ours; he used to come down, we would put one pair in his pocket and he used to keep them shod, so I never had no bother with shoes. He was goodness himself to me; they called him Percy and he would do a pair of shoes at a time for me, and he would take a pair of shoes to the stores if they wanted extra and get them through on his check like that.

**She also explains how she and her husband organised their finances.**

He gave me his whole [wage] packet; he never opened his packet unless there was a collection, and if anybody died and he had no money with him, then he'd open his packet, but he always told me what he'd taken out and take it off his pocket money. If he'd had a good week, well he'd a bit more but we never quarrelled over money, never. And then you started to collect and I could always borrow 'cause he always banked his money; he used to put it in bank for a rainy day - and he was a heavy smoker, I don't know how he managed it but he did.

**Mr Pilgrim's father was wounded in the First World War.**

Money was very scarce because father was shot and wounded very badly in his chest and throat and, although he finished in 1918 when the war finished, he came home to more or less die. So mother was left with six children and she was only twenty-nine. And I remember very well - and this is absolutely true 'cause I've been told so many times in my adult age - that the eldest child got two and sixpence and the children thereafter got two shillings a week as an army pension. I think mother's pension was about twenty-one shillings so six children, plus the rent, rates and whatnot, all had to come out of somewhere around about two pounds ten or something like that. But I suppose, jumping a year or two, at the time when I first thought about it wages were only in the region of two pounds for grown men. That, of course, depends on what sort of job you had; I well remember that my elder brother, who was B.Sc in Chemistry and Physics and was studying then for his Ph.D, was getting three pounds fifteen shillings a week, and the schoolteacher that we knew very well, who lived opposite us, was on four pounds five a week and that was considered a good wage. So you can tell the normal tradesman was getting somewhere about thirty eight bob for a six day week - forty eight hours they worked in those days.

**He also remembers the insurance policies of the time.**

We all had penny insurances in those days, a penny a week. They covered your death, but if you went for fourteen years and you did it like an endowment policy - death or endowment - you'd draw about fourteen pounds; fourteen pounds after fifteen years at a penny a week. We all had penny policies, I can well remember cashing mine. And I remember drawing mother's policy when she died: aye, it was about eleven or twelve pounds or some silly thing like that. But after you'd paid your penny policies for a set number of years you then got a free policy. Even if you finished at fifty and you lived to be eighty you still went to your insurance company which was the Prudential, nearly everybody was in the Pru. You'd go and take your policy and they'd pay you out and, of course, you could get a church service and a choir singing, and a beautiful coffin and a burial and whatnot for thirty pounds.

**Pawnbrokers flourished during hard times.**

Clarence Street, the corner of Colliergate, the corner of Fossgate, in

George Merriman's pawnbrokers in Low Petergate. (Donated to York Oral History Project. Original source unknown.)

Walmgate: you'd see the three balls hanging up and it was chock-a-block. People would say, "If it's a fine day you won't need your raincoat... Off to the pop shop." And you'd get half a crown or two bob and you got a little ticket. When you got your wages they'd sent you off with your ticket and you'd get it back less ten per cent or whatever. If you got two bob for it you'd probably get one and tenpence, so he'd keep tuppence for keeping it for you for two or three days. Sometimes, if you had a big doctor's bill and the doctor wouldn't take it at a shilling a week, you'd go and pawn something that was worth pawning like your wedding ring... I know many people had to do it, and if you had a couple of shillings in your purse on a Thursday night, you know, you were doing well.

**Mr Thomas**

I can say this: although money wasn't very plentiful in those days we never went short of food in any way, but we were not dressed quite as well as we ought to have been. We had to make things last and we had very much repaired things.

Now immediately behind us, of course, was a different class of house and I suppose to some extent the people were not as well off as my father and mother were. I remember a time when regulars used to come, one or two, and she got friendly with quite a number of people in that back street. And they used to come to the back door and say, "Did Mr Thomas bring anything home in his basket?" - in other words, had we any left overs. She sometimes had, sometimes hadn't, but they usually went away with something to eat. They were very, very poor a lot of those people in those houses. I remember Mary, she was a grand girl - she must have been fourteen or fifteen - and she used to come and help mother; she'd scrub her floor and that kind of thing, earn a few coppers, and she'd take us out. Now one day I was missing and my mother said, "Where have you been?" and I said, "I've been with Mary to see her uncle. We've been to see Mary's Uncle George!" "She hasn't got an Uncle George, has she?" "Oh she has, she has that, because I've seen Uncle George; he's got a big shop in York, and he's got a lot of parcels on the shelf!" We'd been to the pawn shop. I didn't know it was a pawn shop!.. It was between Church Street and the Minster on the right hand side and it was fairly well known in York. [The shop was George Merriman's in Low Petergate.] I got to know all about it later. These parcels, of course, were pledges and Mary took a pledge, you see. I learned then, in those days apparently it was the practice for some families who were in straitened circumstances to send the pledges there on Monday morning and recover them on Friday - especially suits, Sunday suits. Well, it must have cost them money to do this; they had tickets and things to get these parcels. Anyway, I'd been with Mary and I was forgiven when mother realised what had happened.

# CHILDREN AND FAMILIES

This chapter views family life from several perspectives. Childhoods are recalled, parental attitudes are discussed, and ways in which boys and girls were treated differently emerge.

### Mrs Armstrong

I was born on Jan 11th 1917 and I lived at the Bar Hotel, Micklegate, which was an old coaching inn I understand. My parents came from Leeds and Pontefract to take it over and I lived there until I was fifteen years old. The rooms were very big which was good for us because we played hide and seek. Our friends liked it very much because we had a large area outside in which we could play. The kitchen was a very large room: all the cooking and eating took place there. We had a nanny called Brownie, and two ladies who came in to help my mother do all the cooking and cleaning both in the house and in the bar area... Brownie's main job was to sort of see we were looked after and able to go to school at the correct time and everything because my mother was too busy. She also took us for days to Scarborough or Brid because our parents couldn't get off for holidays - the hours weren't convenient. The hotel opened eleven am to three pm, then it closed 'till five-thirty, 'till ten-thirty at night, so there was no spare time and it was a seven day a week job... Brownie would arrive about seven-thirty and, incidentally, she would have to walk because there was no transport; the first tram arrived about eight am. And she got breakfast and did something for the rest of the day prior to us going to school because she had to look after us, take us out and that, but when we got to school she would just do odd jobs. Then she helped mother odd times to do baking because at that time it was all baking - everything was home made, there was nothing bought in from shops.

### Did she take you to school?

We were only round the corner, of course. We lived in Micklegate and the school was in Priory Street so we went on our own. There was no problems in that day...you didn't have any fear of anyone really... [We came home for lunch] except for Race Days and it was far too busy. The race crowds used to cross frequently and so we stayed which was a treat; we used to take sandwiches and sit in the playground and eat our lunch, but otherwise we always went home because it was easy... We all had the meal together.

This photograph of Brownie pushing a pram was taken some years after she was Mrs Armstrong's nanny. (Courtesy of Mrs D. Armstrong.)

**And when would she finish? Would she be there in the evening?**
Well, she used to go off, I would say, mostly about six o'clock unless there was any special job they would like her to do. We went to bed early, you see. We weren't late to bed. Even when I left school at fifteen we weren't allowed out.

[Brownie] was there all the time until retirement and we kept in touch until she died - she was eighty odd when she died. She was always an actual person, even when she got older. But everyone was old when they reached forty: everyone looked old, you know, with long skirts and with their hair all done up on top. Mother always wore a long skirt, navy blue.

**How did it feel having a nanny? Did you miss being looked after by your mother?**
Oh, it didn't matter, we enjoyed it really. She wasn't strict but we knew where our place was, you know... Mother was there, it wasn't as if she was away...

**Mrs Hadley**
I was born in July 1918. My father was in the Royal Navy and he had run away from home to join long before World War One. He was brought back and had to wait 'till he was old enough, but he was in the regular navy rather than as a conscript. My mother had been an orphan as a child; an older sister of hers brought her up with her two children who were about the same age, so really my aunt was more like my grandma and we were born in her home. It was in Canon's Gardens, they called it, but shortly

after they moved to 100 Rose Street and it was still war time conditions. I was only about a year when we moved there but I can still remember after the war they had a yard and part of this yard was wired off for hens so they had their own eggs. My first school was Haxby Road and I went there when I was three-and-a-quarter to four, and I can always remember going round the garden there. It always seemed to be warm those days in the spring, I can always remember the lovely chestnut tree with its leaves...

Wives didn't follow their husbands in the Navy as they do now so he decided he would come out - it wasn't fair on my mother or me, you know, not having a husband or father all the time. So he came out in 1922 - I was five then - and they bought a first home in Nunthorpe Road, opposite St Clement's Church.

**Mrs Rennison describes her mother's upbringing.**

Her mother died more or less in childbirth and so she was left at twelve years old with a sister to bring up and so she never really finished her education. She sort of had it hard, really, bringing up a family. There were ten of them altogether and three of them, I think, three girls were taken into the blue-coats or grey-coats, whichever it was. Me mother was the eldest girl and she had...to see to the rest of the family. She spent a whole day washing and a whole day ironing so she didn't really have a lot of life, you know.

**There were many ways in which children were brought up differently in the earlier part of this century. Mrs Armstrong was asked whether most children had pocket money.**

Not a lot. I think we had threepence each which we had to make last all week. I don't think a lot of them got anything; they had to rely on their parents giving them sweets. But, as I say, we had threepence and we bought sweets with it - lots of chewies. We didn't have much else really. I don't remember my mother supplying us with sweets, it were mostly fruit... Bananas, they were very popular, we often used to have those for tea with lovely fresh baked bread and butter; it was lovely because margarine wasn't very well known at that time.

**Miss Beswick**

We didn't get any pocket money! You do a service, you don't get pocket money! The way that I got any pocket money was during the potato picking season; children used to go from the village and they got half a crown for the day. I wanted to do it and mother said, "You can't, Ella, you're not strong enough." However, I pestered them until father let me go to Mr Horner's farm, who was a friend of theirs. One day and I was flat on my back, so he said, "Well, you can pick my potatoes for me and I'll give you sixpence an hour," so I got that. And then we had the golf club at Strensall which is still there - York Golf Club - and you could caddy. They were not very keen on me doing this but they knew I was in the fresh air. A lot of people came from York to caddy, and I caddied for Miss Gloria Preston, the artist who did all those lovely children's things. She always gave me a lift back home in her car; she went the village way to save me walking, and she always gave me sixpence extra. We got a shilling but we had to pay two pence into the club for insurance purposes, so I had one shilling and fourpence. I was about fourteen, I wouldn't have been any younger because mother wouldn't have had me do it. But a lot of the children came out from York to caddy; several of the doctors brought them out in the dicky of their car, and they were poor children, and they used to caddy and they got the money, and the doctors used to give them a jolly good meal - rabbit pie or something like that - so it got them out into the country air.

**Mrs Armstrong's mother also thought that country air would be good for a child.**

When I was three to four - it was because I was an only child, I think, and I wasn't very robust then - they had a friend who worked at the Railway Offices, a farmer's daughter, and my mother decided she would send me to her mother for fresh air, good farm food, eggs and one thing and the other. This daughter - the farmer's daughter - they called her Peach and she lived in York and then on Friday night she would go home for the weekend. We went to a place called Bubwith, then a pony and trap met us and took us to the farm, and things were so primitive there. They had all lamps there and when you went to bed you had a candle. There was no carpets on the floor - all white scrubbed floorboards with rag rugs, hooky rugs. I can remember when we were there, also, we went on a walk to an outlying cottage, and we had the wireless with headphones and we listened at five o'clock to Children's Hour. The other girl had one headphone and I had the other, and it was ever so crackly. That was the first wireless I ever listened to; we didn't have one at home for a long time, but my father bought me a piano, he was ever so fond of music.

**She remembers her father's role in the household and describes the family at mealtime.**

The man of the house was always served first. I was the only one but if there were boys the men were always served first and the boys were always served first. They always had the first cut of meat - that was my first row with my dad. I used to like the outside of the meat - with the first cut the blood run with the knife - and I wanted that outside piece and, of course, it always went on father's plate. I [argued] about it one day and

I was chastised and told my father was the boss of the house and he had preference over anyone.

**Mrs Hadley**

I don't know whether you remember, but if you had egg, poached or boiled, you had one egg but the man of the house had two eggs, and when a boy started work that's when they got two eggs. Soon as he started work he became a man and could have two eggs.

**Was it the same when the girls started work?**

No, usually men were considered more important.

**Mrs Armstrong was asked whether this was accepted at the time.**

They resented it sometimes... I know I did. I was the eldest girl, you see, and he tended to say, "Oh, Richard gets away with it." It was what had to be. My husband was one of a family of nine - five boys, three girls - so it probably wasn't the same in that family because there were too many to argue about. But it was the workers was the most important in the family.

**Did the men help around the house?**

Not many, not as I know anyway. My father in his late years used to wash the windows for my mother [but] not before that because, you see, the wives didn't go out to work so she was expected to do the housework. That's just how it had to be. I don't think many men went shopping either; you seldom saw a man go shopping. My grandad would but I don't think my father ever did.

**Mrs Hadley**

[My father] was very keen. I don't know whether it was because he was in the navy, but before I came to school in the morning he used to have me out in the yard at the back doing Swedish drill and he was very disciplinarian. Oh, very strict but very just. I was never allowed to speak at all, I was brought up on the basis of 'children should be seen and not heard'. I can always remember, we had an old fashioned side-board with glass at the back and my father, mother and I sat facing it. Well, I couldn't help it, there was nowhere else for my eyes to go when I was eating, but my father put brown paper over it because I was vain.

**Mr Armstrong also remembers his father's discipline.**

He was so strict. There was a warning: his chair was in the left hand side of the fireplace, and between the range and the window was a big cupboard...and on the side of the cupboard there was a leather strap and it was hung on a nail and the bottom part of the strap was cut into thirteen thongs. And that was just a warning 'cause he said, "Thirteen's an unlucky

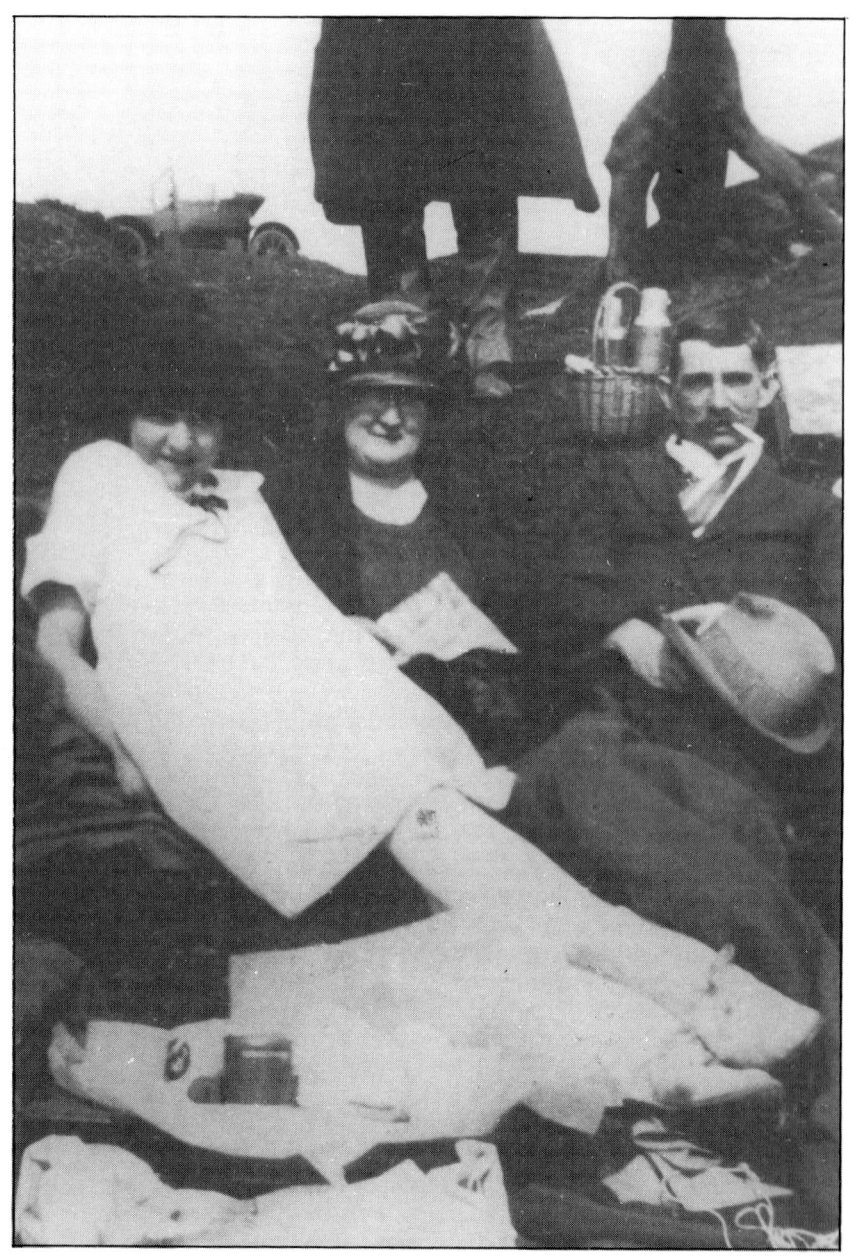

Miss Worfolk with her parents in 1924. (Courtesy of Miss M. Worfolk.)

number, if you get hit with this you're unlucky!" Nobody dared get out of line while that strap was hanging there (and it was always hung there). I only ever saw it used once on one of the brothers, he got a tanning once for something he'd done. He was so strict that not at all did you get out of line; you might outside but not while he was there. We were always there for meals... My father, he fought in the Boer War and also in the first Great War and he was very, very strict. There wasn't a lot of seats in the house, y'know, to sit round the table; we had...a big table [and] when it was open it would be about six feet square, and my father sat at one side with the eldest daughter, and maybe one of the others squeezed in, and then on the other side was a settee which would seat about three. But all the rest...until you were fourteen had to stand to eat, and when you were fourteen you got a seat. That was how strict he was.

**Did you mind?**

No, no, no one minded, you didn't have to mind it was just a rule.

**Mrs Burton was asked if her children ever had any squabbles.**

No, they only had one squabble one morning. Well they used to go to chapel with me every morning and, I don't know, they started fighting about ties or something, and they were running up the house and round the stairs, and they were in a real paddy the both of them. Their father called them in and made them sit down, and he talked to them and made them shake hands, and then he said, "Now you can both go to chapel." I'd gone off and left them in this squabble, I didn't know how they would manage, but he said, "I talked to them, and made them shake hands and be friends." One's nose was bleeding...when they came into chapel - it had been a real fight! It was the only trouble I ever had with them, they were only about nine or ten, I suppose.

**Did your husband spend much time with the children then?**

Yes he did, and he never smacked them and had them at a word. He never, ever smacked them. But they knew when their father spoke, that was it. ...I would say at night, "Go to bed," but they never took any notice of me when I said it was bedtime... But he just had to walk through the door and say, "Allez coucher," and up they went up the stairs, never said a word.

**Miss Beswick's home was also more relaxed than many other households.**

We visited one another's homes. Our home was always open to friends and even to stay the night: if we had been playing hockey and came back my friend would come with me. We'd certainly share my bed; we didn't have a second room or anything, but there was always that. And mother used to put a hot-water bottle in the bed, and very few of the girls had had that done for them - they all used to say how lucky we were.

My father and mother always wanted to know what happened at school during the day, how we'd got on. My father always looked at our homework and they took a great interest in our school... When I got home at night, as I say, we had the hot meal. I finished what homework I had and then, if it was summertime we were allowed to go into the village and go on to the green and play with the other girls, and that. But at the weekend, again, I'd be off for hockey or rounders because I was in the school team, or I had the practice. My sister still jokes to this day about when it was my turn to wash up. I'd say,"Well, I must practise." So I'm afraid I got out of a lot of the domestic chores...but, of course, we made our own beds.

**Mr Thomas came from a large family. He remembers a cradle which was passed around for each new arrival.**

Grandmother had a family of girls, she'd quite a number of them, four or five of them. One lived in Leeds, but all the rest lived in York. There was a cradle, I don't know where it came from but it was a real Moses cradle, wicker-work, with a canopy over the end - quite a good thing I thought. My cousin was a little bit older than me and we shared a lot of time together, and this cradle used to travel round the family, you see - who was having the baby. When the cradle had to go from A to B it was Greg - my cousin Gregory - and I had to take it, and we used to get inside it and put it over our heads and just walk, looking through the wicker-work. It just looked like a sort of tortoise coming. I remember one day we took it from their house or somewhere...and we'd take it down near a pub in Stonegate, and we came out of Stonegate right across in front of St Helen's Square, and into Coney St, and straight down. We had to come over Skeldergate Bridge and from there along the lane where my aunty lived. And we couldn't understand why...these young couples in the pub walked past making such a noise about it, giggling and laughing and shouting and pointing at us, passing rude remarks to each other, and that kind of thing. But that was [the] cradle...we did it several times.

**He also remembers the arrival of twins in the family.**

My parents decided to have more family, must have done. Anyway, they did arrive and they were twins, born in October 1911. I was very perturbed because my mother for quite a time had promised me a pair of trousers, and I was told that these two had arrived. I must have been taken out of the way but I know when I was told my first reaction was, "I shan't get my trousers!" My grandmother heard this story [so] she went home and made me some, but they were short... She made some trousers and she didn't buy new stuff for the job. When I came to look at the trousers closely they had seams in odd places; she'd sewn pieces up together, they were remnants. But they were real tough, hardwearing trousers!

**Miss Worfolk's family owned a draper's shop and she describes the children's clothes they sold.**

I have some old baby clothes. [You] started with a barner, and a binder which was either flannel or cotton, just a straight piece, it went round the baby's tummy. Next they had a vest, a little cross-over one for the tiny babies, usually knitted wool, and then a slip-over for the bigger ones. Then next they had a quilted bodice which slotted through one side and round [and] fastened. I always think it was a good idea because you'd a double thickness of quilting on the baby's back, it helped [give] a bit of support. Then the nappy came, and then a barrycoat which was a long coat which crossed over and was usually flannel. I have one which a friend gave me which she'd made for her son, all beautifully embroidered and scalloped, in blue. Then a long gown, cotton, winceyette, flannel, flannellette, or even nun's veiling which was a wool mixture.

**What colours were they?**

Oh white, no colours! White and cream... Then, of course, a matinee coat, then probably a shawl, and a bonnet always; and there were what we called 'ead squares and they were flannel...embroidered. If it was very cold the end of the barrycoat was turned up, pinned up to make like a little bag to keep the baby a bit warmer. [There were] bibs, of course, but no rubber-backed ones, they were just a bit of winceyette or flannellete at the back. No waterproof pants for the babies. When you took the baby out you had a triangle of cotton, edged with lace, which went over the top of the nappy, which also wasn't much use to keep the water out. No wonder people didn't want to nurse babies in those days!

**The following passages describe how people bathed before they had modern facilities.**

**Miss Kirby was asked if they had a bathroom.**

Oh no! We just had a wash tub. We'd a long tub - a wooden tub - and, of course, we used to put the kettle on, and we got enough hot water that way and then just have it in the bath. With so many of us we always had some clothes, and we used to put the clothes-horse round us and that was full of clothes and you couldn't see one another, it was very nice... Yes, we always were taught to respect privacy and to be careful and thoughtful to one another.

**Mrs Graham**

Well, Friday night...was both bath night and physic night. We had our weekly dose of whatever...was the favourite in your house: ours was the syrup of figs or, I think, castor oil laced with orange juice - every one of them was horrible. But you had to have it, if you didn't you got your nose

A young mother bathes her children outside. (Courtesy of York Castle Museum.)

nipped until you did. Then we had a bath; it was girls on a Friday night and the boys on a Saturday, and there was a few of us, but it was nothing unusual to bath a few friends who happened to be there. My aunt would throw a handful of soda for the last bath to sweeten stuff up, and you were lucky next morning if you didn't wake up with no skin on your back.

**Miss Prentice**

...We had an old bath, me mother got it in a second hand shop, and it were enamelled. It weren't zinc like a lot of them were, it was quite deep and a decent size. It was painted brown outside, white inside, and then on the outside you could see marks where straps had been. Mother had the lid but she never used it. It could be fastened up by straps and could be used for travelling... She used to store it in the back kitchen...on a table to make a bit of room.

**Did you have one night which was bath night?**

We didn't always have it at night, you see. Me dad being getting ready for work it would be in the way, so [we] had to wait and maybe have it in the afternoon.

A travelling bath similar to the one described by Miss Prentice. It has loops for straps and a lockable lid. (Courtesy of York Castle Museum.)

**And how would you heat the water for your bath?**

Well, we had the fire and she had a gas ring in the back kitchen; she used to boil a big panful in these...and a drop of cold to make it decent. She had like a little boiler, like a hob, at the side of the fire and a little brass top to it, it was like a lever: [you] pulled this and water would come out.

**Mrs Rennison**

I remember when we were small we had a sort of oval tin bath-tub, and then as we got older we had one six foot which was a long oval one and that was hung in the yard under the wash-shed. You used to have to bring it in and I think the cleanest went in first. Oh dear, dear, dear, wouldn't we economise if we did it today?

**Miss Beswick**

Oh yes, when we were small father used to help bath us and everything, and carry us up the stairs. Because the bath-house was outside father made an arch so that we were bathed in front of the copper, and he used to put the blanket round us and whisk us up the stairs and into bed.

# HEALTH AND SICKNESS

**The introduction of the National Health Service after the Second World War made an enormous difference to many people's lives. This chapter recalls the days when doctor's bills could cause financial problems, and shows how attitudes towards health care have changed.**

**Mrs Graham brought up a handicapped daughter and she describes how difficult it was for them.**

I was married about two years and Elizabeth was born. We had no idea she was handicapped for about three years...and it was rather hard then because...nobody seemed to know - they didn't do much in that way with spastics, I don't think they understood... [She was born on] July 23rd 1942, right in the middle of the war. I was pushed around, seeing where I could get help... If you'd anyone handicapped when Elizabeth was young there were a lot of people who feared you; they didn't mean to but they avoided you because I think they were frightened they might get involved. Then we got her fixed up and, as you know, now it's a very helpful world [with] no need for anyone to feel it's just happened to them because it's not that way at all.

**Do you have other children?**

I have a daughter, Kathleen - everything was very straightforward there. I think, really, Elizabeth was a legacy of the war. She was born after an air raid: I was frightened, very frightened indeed, and I felt as if something had gone off inside me and I never felt her anymore. The specialist at the hospital said, "You tell me what you attribute it all to...mothers are rarely ever wrong." He said that if she'd been born at seven months - the air raid was in April - she would probably have been quite normal, but she took the shock...

I think medical science was just having a bit of a recess, and I think it was a public attitude [that] if they had a [spastic] child they didn't want anyone to know - you sort of blamed yourself. I know my husband's mother was deeply shocked, she used to say, "There's never been anything in my family, Clare." And I said, "I don't know if there has in mine." But I mean, now nobody blames anybody at all, it just happens doesn't it? And she's brought a lot of happiness. I would have loved her normal, of course, but I wouldn't like taking away from me what she's learned me - we're still happy.

**Mrs Burton lived in a village and she describes the lack of modern facilities.**

The only water we had was a pump outside with a big well under the washhouse. Every kettle and everything, we'd to go outside, and the water wasn't pure, you know, it was just in a well and it was never cleaned out or anything. But, I mean, it was the same all over the village and I suppose we didn't get things because we were full of germs so we were immune to them!

**She also recalls how she helped her neighbours during times of illness.**

I looked after the children myself... But there was someone across the road had dropsy and she was very ill a long time. They'd no children and the husband was always coming for me to go and sit with her and look after her. I mean, she wasn't a friend, it was just being a neighbour, that was all... He would often come about two o'clock for me in the night and I had to get up and go to her. She was very ill, mind you, but I don't know why he sort of called me - being next door I suppose. And then in the morning he used to say, "Will you stop while I just milk the cows?" while I wanted to be home seeing to the children. But I had to stay, you had to stay... In the village, I mean everyone would help if anyone was very ill. I used to take the butcher's baby [because] when she was born he had consumption. I used to take the baby for the day - a very new baby - while her husband was ill. It's a bit of an effort taking a tiny baby but I loved babies and I used to help anybody in the village if they had a baby because I loved it.

**Mrs Rennison also remembers how neighbours helped out.**

We didn't have the community services that we have now, and if Mrs So-and-so was ill then Mrs So-and-so down the street would go in for a couple of hours and clean for her. I don't suppose there was much money at it because people hadn't the money but there was more community spirit I think.

**Mr Pilgrim recalls how much work was done by the district nurse.**

I remember the district nurse very well indeed. Ninety out of a hundred births it was the district nurse who officiated and only called the doctor in if things were sadly wrong. Another thing they used to do, they used to come to school. I don't know whether it was once a month or something like that, but everyone had to kneel down and put your head on her lap on a sheet and she'd go through your hair to see if you had any vermin in it. I suppose half the class had got them, particularly the girls because of their long hair. You always knew because she came and gave you a little note; if you went away without a little note you were OK. If you got a note it was to your parents telling them to wash your hair in paraffin or [something], but I think you could go down to the hospital and produce the note and they used to give you a tub of black looking slimy ointment which you rubbed on your head. I remember our mother used to comb our hair with what they call a toothcomb: they had very, very fine teeth on both sides. She used to get a sheet of paper or linen, duck your head down, comb your hair, and look in the comb to see if there were any little white blobs which they called nits. I don't know what they called the other things. Mother used to comb, and comb, and comb to us all!

**A formal photograph of a traditional hospital ward. (Donated to York Oral History Project.)**

**He also remembers the days before the National Health Service when doctor's fees had to be paid.**

Now I went into the County Hospital and a lady came round and asked you a lot of questions, and then they would say, "Well, how much can you afford to pay?" I said, "I don't know, you'll have to ask my mother."
...Every visit to the doctor you paid, and that was anything from two shillings to three shillings a visit - a lady used to come round and collect your money. If he'd come half a dozen times you paid it at a shilling a week or two bob a week; she used to come round on Friday night and pick up the cash. So you avoided being ill or avoided calling the doctor; but, of course, chickenpox [and things like that] was a notifiable disease

so you'd got to call the doctor who would inform the Local Authority - that's how you got taken away.

...If you went to the doctor...you would then have to go and buy a bottle of medicine or whatever it was, so in consequence of that you had a lot of old women's cures. You never went to the doctor if you could possibly help it. Now if the doctor came to you, many times he would charge you five bob or seven and six, or something like that. Well, you couldn't afford to pay seven and six out of two pounds...so he had [this] lady coming round the district.

**Mr Thomas describes how families got medicine in his area.**

...If families round about wanted any medicine - of course, we didn't have National Health in those days - they had to go to Canon Argles' house and he gave them a dispensary note that enabled them to go to the dispensary, which was in Duncombe Place, and get medicine made up at no cost.

**Mrs Burton talks about childcare when she was a young mother.**

They used to go to bed very early. The first year we used to have them in bed at four and get them up at seven for their meal - a bottle, I never fed any of them, they had milk. They were very tiny. I was in bed three months with my eldest son, and there was nothing the matter with him, but I just had nothing to eat. He weighed about two pounds and a half which, of course, today... He should have been in an incubator, you see. But anyway, we fed him with a fountain pen filler every two hours, night and day, because he was just starved to death, he was just like those little pigs that die... He was just skin and bone, but nothing the matter with him at all... Of course, when the other two children were coming I dieted all the time. I didn't have any meats and I kept going. But with my first one I didn't understand. It was a friend in York, she said to me, "Your face is swollen, isn't it?" I said, "No, I don't think so." And I looked... and I said, "Well, I'll see the doctor tomorrow." I saw him the next day and he just put me to bed, and I was never up any more. Just used to have cream crackers and soup.

**Mr Pilgrim's description of scarlet fever in the family shows how rapidly healthcare has changed.**

I can remember the whole family, excepting mother and myself, got scarlet fever and in those days it was almost a crime! You sent for the health authorities and they used to wrap you in a blanket, and people would get away from your house - walk on the other side - because you'd got scarlet fever. You used to go into isolation and the Isolation Hospital was on Huntington Road. You went into isolation because you had scarlet fever, and you came out and you'd find they'd got scabies - you know, sores all over - that they'd picked up from the sheets that someone had had in another part of the hospital and hadn't been properly washed. And the kids picked it up so they went back again and then they got whooping cough - and I escaped the lot! I used to go along Huntington Road and stand at the gates and wave to them through the window. They were there for six weeks.

...Two workmen with masks would come and they would seal the doors and fumigate all through the bedrooms and through the house. This horrible van would come up the front - you know, fumigation - and it was almost a crime to get those things.

**Mrs Armstrong and Mrs Hadley recall the days before modern dentistry.**

**Mrs Hadley**

Do you remember the old Dental Clinic in Piccadilly, the wooden hut? There was a wooden hut in Piccadilly - oh so primitive! You used to go from school...and you used to hear the screams coming from inside. You just went in and they yanked your teeth out.

**Mrs Armstrong**

If there was anything wrong it came out, it just came out. When I left school and got a job I went to a dentist, and when the dentist offered to fill me a tooth I was a little bit sceptical about it, I thought usually they pull them out... We never thought of having our teeth filled. My mother, she had her teeth out very early in life because that's how they did it.

**Mrs Hadley**

And if they weren't very well... My mother wasn't very well when she was about twenty one, I understand, [and] she went to the hospital for something - this is only hearsay - and she had all her teeth out in the hope it would make her better. Actually, I think she did become stronger then, but I don't think it was a question of her having bad teeth, it was just a question of they thought she would.

# CHRISTMAS

Christmas has always been a time when families unite in the home. In this short chapter people recall various aspects of a traditional Christmas.

**Mrs Rennison**

I can remember one particular Christmas when me brother was born. He was born on the 22nd December and I always said Father Christmas brought him because I saw Father Christmas - but I can't remember how me parents taught me that there is no Father Christmas. I always remember that Christmas: one of my aunts had brought me a pot tea service - the teapot was in the shape of a rabbit. There were three of us in four years so I'd only be three going onto four, perhaps, when he was born and I got this tea pot service. Me brother, the middle one, he was two and when he saw this tea service that was all he wanted, and I can remember me father saying, "Well, when the shop's open again we'll get you one, you can't have that." Christmas in those days was just two days, not a week and a half, or a fortnight like it is now, and I can remember me father going to Woolworth's and buying this little tin Mickey Mouse tea service - looking back, Mickey Mouse must have been very young in those days. I can remember one Christmas having twin dolls and a dolls pram - as I say, we weren't deprived of things like that. Our next door neighbour worked at Rowntree's and he was able to buy waste, and...one Christmas he came in and he'd painted us all a tin with our name on which we thought was absolutely marvellous 'cause we didn't get a lot of sweets in those days.

**When people had less money to spend, Christmas was inevitably different as Miss Beswick recalls.**

We didn't have a lot of presents like children do today, but as a small child...we always had a stocking, and there was the orange, and the apple, and the nuts, and the sugared mouse, and usually some money in wrapping-up paper; and then perhaps one...like a book, or perhaps when we were smaller a toy, but we used to make our own toys. We always had a proper Christmas dinner, you know, turkey and whatever mum had made - the Christmas cake, and the plum pudding. Nothing was bought, the mince pies and everything she made. We all used to have to stir the pudding and the cake, it was a tradition to do that. And we had our holly and things, and we had our Christmas parties - we had friends in for Christmas parties.

We used to have a game, 'Pass the Ring', and then we had, 'The Grand Old Duke of York', I remember singing that.

**Miss Kirby also remembers Christmas dinner and she describes a sauce her mother made.**

Mother could always - I don't know how she managed it - but she could always work out a bit of something special. I don't ever remember having turkey or anything like that, we didn't do as much as that, but probably she managed a chicken or she used special meat. And we always had a Christmas pudding. Oh, we had mother's home-made sauce, very highly seasoned - there was so much in that it made it brown. It was white sauce but it was brown. I loved it. There was ginger, nutmeg, cinnamon and what else was in? There was about four things and a lot of sugar. It was gorgeous! And she made a lovely pudding with lots of fruit in. We started about mother's birthday - which was fifth of October - to begin to get in for Christmas. She would get a few extra currants, and we also got some extra soap and things like that, so that...she hadn't to spend her money on cleaning things when she wanted to spend her money on fruit and things for Christmas.

**Baking for Christmas was always special.**

**Mrs Graham**

Before the Christmas cake was made we had to go out into the Fulford fields and find a very long piece of stick, a chunky piece of wood. [The cake was baked] in one of these black ranges and gradually you put it in bit by bit - the cake was there, the stick was out here - and, of course, that lasted most of the evening. You only need a low fire and you pushed it under gradually; for hours you couldn't mend the fire properly...and we were frozen to death sometimes.

**Mrs Armstrong was asked if Christmas puddings were boiled in the wash copper.**

That's right, in the wash-copper, then bring them in and hang them to drip and then they were ready for Christmas. They were done about a fortnight before but cakes were done much earlier. There were always these 'tasters' and even when we were married my mother and sister used to bake and there was always a 'taster' of their Christmas cake to see if it was alright. What would have happened if it wasn't I don't know... We used to chop candied peel with the sugar on it. [You had] half an orange and candied it with sugar, and then when it was set the sugar was solid in the cup with the orange or lemon or lime. Then you cut all these little bits up - you know how you get chopped peel now? Well, you chopped this by yourself.

A selection of old toys, cards, and decorations. (Courtesy of York Castle Museum.)

**Mr Thomas remembers other aspects of Christmas in York.**

Well my father, being a countryman, used to observe country practice... I don't remember seeing a gooseberry often, or a turkey, but my mother was always partial to ducks and big chickens for the main meal. Then Christmas Eve and New Year's Eve we used to have 'frummarty', as they called it. That was boiled wheat and there was ginger in it, and I believe black treacle and that kind of thing. My father had a ceremony of putting the Yule log on the fire [and] on Christmas morning...we always got a nice present from our next door neighbour. [We had] Yule candles and the youngest one had to light the Yule candles, I think, from the Yule log. I think that was the way it went. When it got to midnight I had to go out and bring in some green, knock on the door, and be admitted, and that kind of thing, and be given a glass of ginger wine or something like that. I was chosen because I was the dark one - my brother was very, very fair. There was an awful lot of fruit about which we bought in the York market - it was a very good market... Anyway, there were stalls, and at night time they used to have a flare going, hanging down - paraffin things. And you could get small oranges at Christmas time, you could get them twenty-four for a shilling. Apples, of course, were plentiful, bananas less plentiful, but any home-grown stuff, there was quite enough of that. And you always took home a bunch of holly round about that time; they used to put the bits of holly over the picture frames and that kind of thing.

**Mrs Thomlinson's recollection of Christmas reveals the generosity of the community she grew up in.**

Every street had a corner shop in Leeman Road practically, and I used to go round on a Boxing Day and they always used to give us an orange and a Christmas box. Where you shopped most (that was just in our street) they gave us a threepenny bit. I can remember being sat surrounded in oranges and apples, and we used to get quite a few nuts as well. I can always remember we used to roast chestnuts.

**Mrs Hadley remembers Christmas decorations.**

I can always remember at Christmas, Boyes' shop always had the most beautiful windows: fairies flying around, a Cinderella, or Goldilocks and three bears - you just went to see the window. There were no moving things. Leake and Thorpe started it but Boyes' was the main one I think. We always had a Christmas tree. Actually, my Christmas tree lasted forty-nine years; my mother bought it in Halifax - an artificial tree - when I was three. I was longing to keep it fifty years but every year it was going, and my husband kept saying, "This won't go up another year," and after forty-nine years, that was it. We had a Victorian bauble - still have it - silver with knobs on, and that was always too heavy to go on the tree. It looked very real, it was made of goose feathers twisted round so it looked exactly like a fir tree.

**Mrs Armstrong**

We had beautiful baubles and decorations and things to go on the tree... They were lovely times.

# GAMES AND ENTERTAINMENT

Another aspect of family life which has been changed dramatically by new technology is entertainment. This chapter recalls how children and families spent their leisure time before televisions and modern equipment were widely available.

**Mr Pilgrim explains a game they played when he was a boy.**

A game we used to love to play - of course it was only summer playing - was 'peggy'. You got a piece of wood about six inches long and about the round of a cricket stump, and you shaved the ends off until it was shaped so that when you put it on the ground you could tap one end and it span into the air. Then, if you were lucky you'd a cricket stump, if you weren't lucky you'd just got a piece of wood, and there was a team out in the field and the other team stood on your left - same as they play rounders today. You used to tap the front of it and it span into the air, and then you used to take a swale at it, you know. Some of them were so expert they could knock it fifty, eighty yards with just a piece of wood. Now if you were caught, of course, you were out, but if you weren't caught you ran like the clappers between two points. We usually liked to play in a lane because they were so dangerous were those things and they'd go through somebody's window like nobody's business. We used to play in the lane between Vyner Street and Fountain Street, quite a broad lane where the horse and carts used to go, and we used to play that for hours. Then they used to hear a voice, "Are you there Butch?" - this was the brother - "Well it's dinner time and if you don't get you'll get your ears boxed." We all disappeared in for our dinners then, nobody knew the time. It was only when somebody shouted that you went in because I don't suppose one in a thousand school kids had a watch, whereas I don't suppose one in a thousand hasn't got one now.

**Mrs Thomlinson remembers playing games in the Leeman Road area.**

Oh yes, there were a lot of games in Leeman Road... We'd throw the ball up at the lovely big wall at the end house; I often wondered how they stuck us but they never grumbled. And hop-scotch we played, we always had a game. And then we played with a scrap-book: we used to have scraps in books and stick a pin in, and if you got a page with a scrap you had to give the scrap up. You know, I have a big thick book today.

**Did you get those things from magazines and comics?**

No, you'd to buy scraps in sheets. Some girls only put half a dozen in a big thick book but if you were a bit lenient you put more scraps in and you lost them.

I also liked dolls. People must have been a bit sorry for us without a dad because I had another auntie who took me to Marks and Spencer's when it was 'penny bazaar', and as you walked in there was every doll you could think of on the left, it was lovely. I can always remember picking a lovely little baby doll, and I can also remember buying little celluloid dolls for a penny or tuppence... I used to love going shopping there.

Four York children on bicycles. (Courtesy of Mrs E. Guyll.)

**Mrs Rennison describes her first bicycle.**

I remember getting my first bike, when I was about twelve, which was one of those second-hand sit-up bikes. Oh dear, I had all on reaching the pedals but it was great: somebody had done it up and painted it black and I felt I was the bee's knees.

I had quite a lot of fun with there being a lot of children in the street. Fighting did go on, I suppose, at times, but I remember particularly in the winter time 'cause we seemed to have more snow in those days. We used to build walls in the snow where you could have snow ball fights with the kids in the next street; no wilful damage was done like there is today, we were just happy. Oh, you'd call it a snowball fight, but I don't think it got to a nasty stage.

**Mrs Graham describes one of the ways she spent her evenings at home.**

We had a sort of frame thing and often on a night you'd cut up old cloth, washed coats and things, to make those pricked-rugs with pretty patterns. We'd all sit round... You had a thing like a comb with a sharpened end, and then you backed them with hessian. They were very nice, nice to your feet, but they did hold the dirt.

**Mr Pilgrim's family also stayed together.**

In the winter evenings we spent quite a lot of time playing cards and tiddley-winks - three or four nights a week - it was a sort of family gathering. But perhaps we kept together more because we hadn't a father and we all had a feeling of sympathy towards mother.

**Mr Thomas was not allowed to play cards.**

Well, my father was rather against cards and consequently I'm completely ignorant about [them]. I can't play cards today, not ordinary playing cards. He was very, very cross and he used to say, "I'm not having cards in this house. Wherever there's cards [there's] trouble!" And that was that. But we did play other games: snakes and ladders, ludo, and things like that. We also had plasticine to play with and we used to draw. We played outdoor games like leap-frog, but nothing that involved spending money, I mean buying equipment.

A young girl does a jigsaw while her mother knits by the fire. (Courtesy of Rowntree's Archives.)

**The next two passages describe a custom at weddings which obviously provided great entertainment for local children.**

### Mr Armstrong

One of the things I can remember about...weddings in those days: they used to throw coins out of the window to the youngsters - all the families did it. They used to warm some coins up on a shovel over the fire (you know, ha'pennies and pennies) and they used to take them up into the bedroom, open the window, and they used to throw them out. All the youngsters used to scramble for them down below and as soon as they got hold of them they used to drop them again because they were quite hot sometimes.

### Mrs Thomlinson

Saturday afternoons as children was watching weddings; we used to stand outside, wait for bride to go in, and when she came out we used to run like billyo to chapel. We lived in the street where the chapel was and after the wedding they always used to put pennies on over this fire and throw them out for the kids. They were red-hot pennies and nobody could hold them long....and that to me was so happy to be married like that.

### Why did they heat them on the fire ?

I don't know, I suppose it was when you picked them up you dropped them and another child got them, you see.

### Mrs Armstrong and her brother both played musical instruments.

My brother played the mandoline, I had the piano, and my sister was to be taught the violin but she didn't like it and I don't think she took any lessons... There was a man used to come and he gave [my brother] lessons, but I used to go to this lady's house to be taught because I didn't want it at school; I think it was because I was the only one who had to practise.

My first piano was pretty ancient, but when I was fifteen my mother had an insurance policy for me - everyone took out an insurance policy for their children, usually at the age of one - and it was due when I was fifteen. She bought me a new piano with it - well, it was new to me - and it was one of the small type. I kept it until 1957, or was it 1958? When I used to play it the dog used to howl so I got rid of the piano, perhaps I should have got rid of the dog, I don't know.

### Miss Beswick's family also had a pet.

Uncle George had brought two [parrots] from Africa...and he gave one to my father. Now ours was a very good talker, [he did] my father's voice exactly. If you were not in the room you wouldn't know whether it was him or not... I know it was one chore that we never quarrelled over as children: we all had to go over to the pit to get sand for the cage, and we took it in turns (week in, week out) for getting Polly's sand and cleaning the cage out. We had her for about twenty years, and she died of the Spanish 'flu.

She would call us all by name and strange to say, after my brother left us to go to Bradford we never heard him call, "Richard!" again.

**He knew which one was which?**

Oh yes. And when the boys were going off to cricket and were just sidling off, the parrot used to call, "Richard! George!" and back they'd come and say, "Yes father? Why, what's the matter? We were just going to play cricket." That blessed parrot. We used to get so cross with it...

**Mrs Armstrong remembers the radios they used to have and Mr Armstrong explains how they were run.**

**Mr Armstrong**

[There was] no electricity, the radio ran from accumulators; you had to go to the shop to get it charged. We went to Dennis Chalk's which was just round the corner; he had a big shop in Goodramgate but he just had a little shop to repair radios and re-charge. They used to last about a fortnight. We had two and while one was being used the other was being charged up.

**Mrs Armstrong**

...Everyone came to listen to our radio and you had to have a proper licence to transmit it to public rooms, so to avoid that my father used to stand it on a table at the door into the living room and everyone used to cluster round the bar to listen to the radio. It had two programmes, I think Daventry was the main one. It used to rattle and carry on really but they were so thrilled with it - we had that one for some time. The next radio we had from Cussins and Light, it was relay, and we paid so much a week for it.

**Mr Armstrong**

They just wired from chimney to chimney like a telephone.

**Mrs Graham remembers going to the cinema.**

We went to the Rialto Cinema - we called it the Flea Pit - and we used to start off about two o'clock right at the front. Before we were through at night we'd seen three performances but we'd gradually graduated to the best seats, and we did it like that!

This advertisement appeared in the Yorkshire Evening Press in 1938.
(Courtesy of York Castle Museum.)

**Mrs Moore preferred the theatre.**

I don't think I ever went to the pictures, I can't remember. The children went Saturday mornings - penny was it? They used to go on a cheap ticket when they were older and could go by themselves but I never went to the pictures, I hadn't the time. I loved the theatre, we used to have block bookings for the theatre before we were married - gangway seats in the stalls every Saturday. I used to see every musical comedy which came to York, it was lovely; but I never went after, I couldn't afford it.

**Mrs Armstrong also enjoyed the musical comedies.**

With father we used to go to the theatre when the musical comedies were on: *Mr Cinders, No, No Nanette, Lilac Time*. There used to be quite a lot of Schubert, but we used to like that. It was a big thing going to the theatre. After I left school I used to be very fond of ballet. If ever the ballet came - oh, and Gilbert and Sullivan too - and if ever the D'Oyly Carte came, we used to go in the gods. That was primitive: plain wood and very dusty with straight wooden bars. I always said you could hear the music better up there. My friends didn't seem to go but on the other hand you always seemed to go with your parents. I always used to go with my mother and father.

**Mr Pilgrim describes some family excursions in York.**

We didn't travel far because we'd got no means of travelling - we just couldn't afford to travel - but we had our little excursions as a family. For instance, I can well remember every Easter the family went to Acomb with Easter eggs which had been boiled and coloured by tea or coffee, or painted, and go and roll them down the slope on Acomb Green. Well that to us, oh it was marvellous. We went on the tram all the way and played about there, and then came back again. Whitsuntide we would probably go to the Homestead, but one of the biggest treats of the year was to go on what was called 'Black Harry's Gunboat': this was *The River King* that went from King's Staith to Bishopthorpe and back. It was one of those steam things, you know, with lots of smoke coming out of the funnel, and that was another treat. But several times we used to get the tram to the corner of Gillygate and walk down to Marygate to the river, with sundry stops, and finish up at the Homestead and have a picnic. We'd wander wearily home from there. Everything was done as youngsters together and mum coming with us.

**Mrs Moore also went to the Homestead when she was a child and she explains how she got there.**

Through ferry boat: it was a penny, or a ha'penny if you was under five... There was about twenty four houses in Albany Street - and then there was another street at the top had one or two - and we used to collect. There'd be eight or ten children - we couldn't take many because the boat wouldn't hold too many. It was an old-fashioned boat and we used to meet the night before and say, "If the weather's fine in the morning meet such and such a time." We used to meet at half past nine/quarter to ten. "Don't forget to bring your dinners and don't forget your pennies for the ride in the thing." When he'd taken us over and seen us safely onto bank...we used to just walk up to Homestead and used to play games, and there was a sand pit and a little play park. It was a lovely park and there was a thing with monkeys in, and birds.

**Mrs Armstrong remembers St George's Fair.**

My father, he always used to take us to St George's Fair, you know, when the fair came... He used to throw for the coconuts more than going on the rides - I think they were a little bit chilly those rides - and he used to throw coconuts to win something. They had something called the Lusitania which had very big swing-boats all netted in: there was two, and one came up as the other came down. Then there was the horses which were very big, splendid and colourful. Then there was the Cakewalk which shook, and the Chairoplane. I was always a bit timid about going on anything but I did go on the Cakewalk, I remember. And, of course, in those days they had the boxing booths: they offered them to go and fight their boxers, didn't they? It wasn't quite as noisy as the present day ones. I know there were noises there, but they were more of an organ, musical type of thing, with steam organ and figures ringing bells.

**Mr Thomas remembers York Gala, an annual event which many people enjoyed.**

We all sat up there on these carts and we were taken to what was known as the 'Gala Field' which was on Bootham Park. There we had all sorts of interesting sports - fire balloons and things of that sort - and had a jolly good time too. We had to take our own mugs and we were handed enormous bags of buns and things when we got there, and plenty of tea out of big tea-pots - they were enormous, like kettles. Every year York florists used to organise the Gala: I believe they were what you call The Horticultural Society and they were very keen. The flower show was a feature of the Gala, they held it every year. They used to have an enormous marquee in Bootham Park grounds with all the exhibits in there, but that wasn't of great interest to me. I used to get to the Gala every year because my uncle, a publican in York, used to get tickets for displaying posters. We used to get these passes and away we used to go, my cousin and I. And, of course, one of the great things was the balloons, the gas balloons: they used to have two of them, one filling and one ready, and they were filled with ordinary town gas which was generated in Layerthorpe in the gas

**York Gala in Bootham Park as seen from one of the gas balloons. (Courtesy of York Castle Museum.)**

works. Captain Spencer looked after the airships, 'The Aeronaut' we called him. He'd be sitting in baskets with bags of sand all around and the balloon up over the top. There was a big hose tied to a steam engine (it was some kind of traction engine) and the balloon used to go up and down - it was five shillings a time. Well, there was great excitement one day when the holder broke... I wasn't actually at the Gala at the time, but I was with the lads running down the street crying, "Balloon's broke away! Balloon's broke away!" And sure enough it was there, it was sailing very, very steadily with a great long line hanging down, not touching the ground, of course. But it sailed away, it went north-east I think.